CANADIAN FRONTIER

ANNUAL

**Edited by Brian Antonson
with contributions from 26
Canadian writers.**

PRINTED IN CANADA

Nunaga Publishing

© **Nunaga Publishing Company Ltd., 1976**
and individual authors

Nunaga Publishing Company Ltd.
Editorial Office: 12165 - 97th Avenue
                 Surrey,
                 British Columbia

ISBN 0-919900-14-3
ISSN 0315-0062

Printed in Canada by
D.W. Friesen & Sons
Altona, Manitoba

Canadian Shared Cataloguing in Publication Data

Main entry under title:

Canadian frontier

    Quarterly, 1972-75; annual 1976-
    Imprint varies.
    ISSN 0315-0062

    1. Frontier and pioneer life - Canada -
Periodicals.
FC1.C35   971'.0405
F1001.C

WELCOME

Welcome to 112 pages of the most exciting History you might ever come across: Canada's.

From the time the first men moved down from the Bering Sea crossing into the heartland of Canada, through the visits by pioneering Norsemen, the early establishments by 16th Century French explorers, the expansion of the British stronghold, and right up to present-day world power, exciting events have shaped the path of our country. And through those many, many years, the stories of our country's growth have been passed from generation to generation.

Today, as at no time before in our country, there is a new awareness of what has been, and a growing demand for more insight into the past that is our heritage. More and more Canadians are finding themselves trapsing to library and newspaper office to delve into the pages of our history. More and more Canadians are chronicling these events from the past, bringing a new and vibrant life to what has gone before. From such people, we have gleaned twenty-seven glimpses of our heritage—twenty-seven unique capsules that show the character and timbre of our foundations, twenty-seven tales of yesterday: researched, written and presented with authenticity, accuracy and factuality uppermost in mind.

Our stories cover the breadth of our great country, for as each new section was opened to the chronicler's pen, fresh events took place that made meat for hungry historians. Perhaps the east dominates: but it was ever thus. The New World was approached by European man from the east, and the west was populated last. The east has had more time to acquire a history—when the west was yet unexplored, the War of 1812 was raging on the Niagara Peninsula. When the rebellion of 1837 was occupying the news in Upper Canada, the possibility of the Riel Rebellions in the latter half of the century was very remote indeed. But as our west grew, writers put down facts and fictions for later readers, and from these accounts have come some of the works you hold now.

CANADIAN FRONTIER Magazine was established in 1972 to provide a much-needed forum for historical journalism. Through the years, it has matured and grown. Perhaps the chroniclers of OUR age will look upon it as an attempt to establish a voice for Canada's past—an attempt at which it has succeeded admirably. The CANADIAN FRONTIER BOOK ANNUAL is an outgrowth of the former quarterly magazine, brought about by many things: economic pressures, production pressures, and the lack of strong government support and encouragement for the periodical publishing of such magazines in Canada today. Our attempt to make CANADIAN FRONTIER an effective voice in a quarterly format has met these frustrations head-on for some time now, but the opportunity has appeared to make the publication an ANNUAL one, and we're taking advantage of it. This book, containing some of the most interesting and exciting accounts of Canadian history, will provide excellent reading for the avid history fan and for the serious student of days gone by.

We urge you to let yourself go as you delve into your history. Immerse yourself in the struggles of our pioneers, in the battles of forgotten wars, in the simple pleasures of pioneer life, in the legends that have a basis somewhere—but where?

Pull up your favorite chair, let the dog out, light the fire, stir a warm drink, set yourself down, and enjoy.

Good reading!

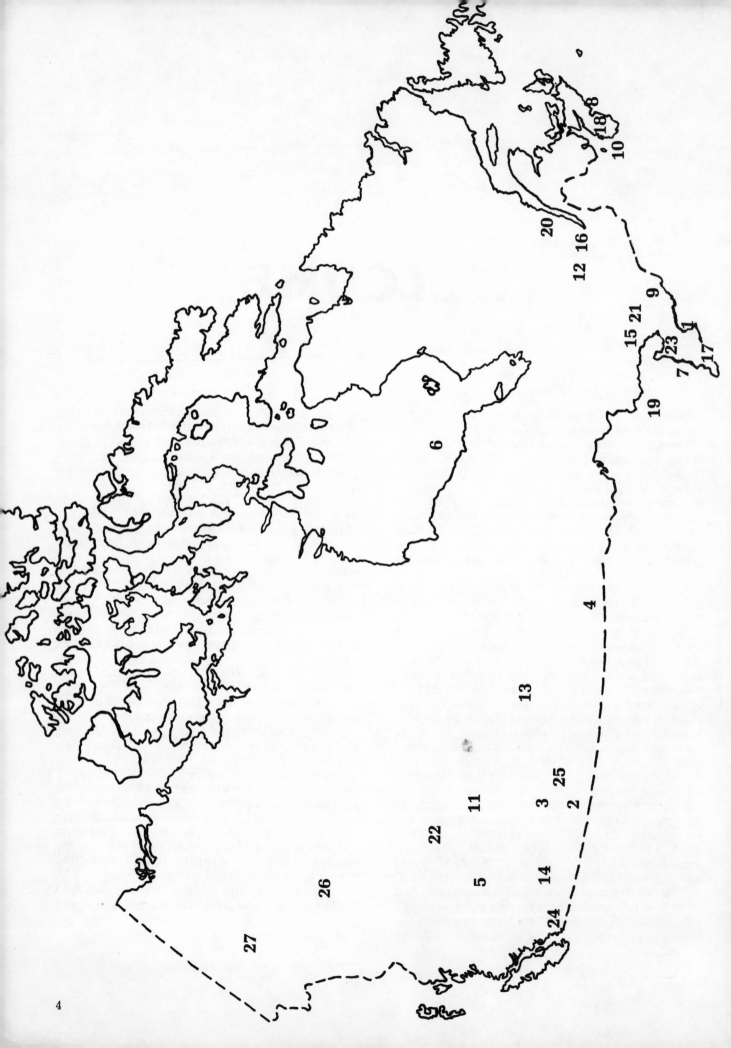

CONTENTS

TIGER IN THE FOREST

Fitzgibbon of the 49th.

by Hugh F. Cochrane

In June of 1813 he donned the coarse clothing of a farmer and went to mingle among the 1,500 U.S. troops setting up their camp on the western end of Lake Ontario. The disguise covered his tall muscular frame and a slow shuffle gave him an appearance much older than his 33 years. From a basket hung on his arm he sold blocks of butter to the troops, yet all the while his steel-grey eyes probed every detail of the camp. He noted the tents of the officers, the placement of artillery along the edge of a shallow ravine and the areas patrolled by sentries. Each step took him deeper into the enemy camp and all the while he half expected to hear at any moment a sharp command to halt, or to feel the hard muzzle of a musket against his ribs.

When he had gathered the information he had come for, he turned to retrace his steps to the road that led from the camp. Instead he found himself looking directly into the stern faces of a group of American officers who had moved in to block his retreat. There was no doubt in his mind that he could be shot as a spy. Even so, there was no fear or any sign of emotion on his weathered features, only the pleased expression of a backwoods settler who had managed to sell some of his produce.

As the officers came closer he stopped and held up his basket as if to offer his goods for sale. But they had not come to buy and one of the officers rudely brushed the basket aside while another demanded that he tell them what he knew about British troops in the area.

The man's weathered features broke into a grin; still playing the part of the ignorant settler pleased that officers of such high rank had stopped to talk to him. Troops? Yes. He had seen quite a few in the last day or so. They had passed by with their

Troops? Yes. They were going this way and that and they seemed to be in a hurry.

muskets. They were going this way and that and they seemed to be in a hurry. As if running from something. He wasn't sure where they had went. He had his work to do and he hadn't paid much attention.

The officers were frustrated with the lack of information in his answers and further questions brought nothing of value. They became impatient and finally turned away mumbling about this ignorant clod of a farmer who knew so little about military affairs.

He waited for a moment as they walked away, then resumed his slow shuffle as he made his way out of the camp. In the afternoon sun he was a shabby figure on a dusty road that few would bother to glance at. Yet, unknown to those in the camp, there was far more to this clod of a farmer.

At 17 he had left his native Ireland to serve the British Crown. At 18 he had fought along side of Brock and Sheafe during the invasion of Europe. He had led his men over the sand dunes in Holland and into the blazing guns of Napoleon's army and he had suffered winter marches and tortures in French prison camps. He had seen his comrades fall around him and he had shivered in Baltic winds on the deck of the same ship as Lord Nelson.

In a word, Lieutenant James Fitzgibbon of the 49th

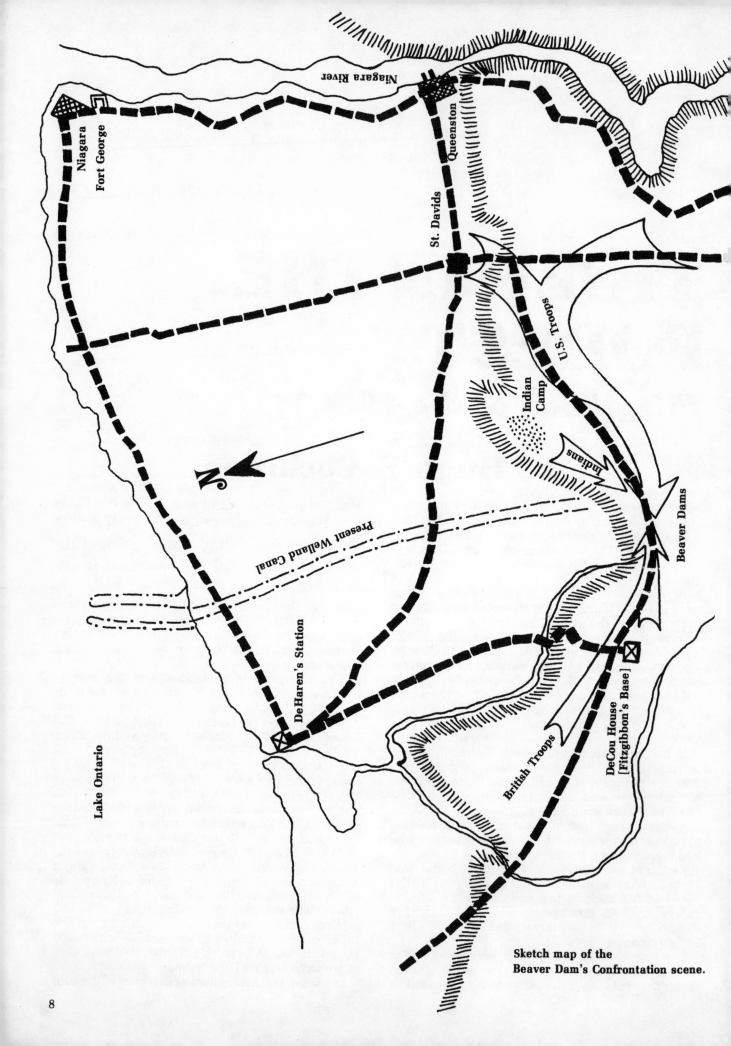

Niagara River

Niagara
Fort George

Queenston

St. Davids

U.S. Troops

Indian Camp

Indians

Beaver Dams

N

Present Welland Canal

DeHaren's Station

British Troops

DeCou House
[Fitzgibbon's Base]

Lake Ontario

Sketch map of the
Beaver Dam's Confrontation scene.

regiment, the famed "Green Tigers", had come up the hard way. In his 18 years of service he had faced death many times and, like General Brock his commanding officer, he had earned the respect of the men who served under him. Although they didn't know it yet, those same American officers would meet this coarse-clad figure again, but under far different circumstances. For this "Green Tiger" had a score to settle for the death of his commander General Isaac Brock whom the Americans had killed at Queenston Heights several months before. Even now as the shabby figure melted into the shadows along the road the shuffle which he had used in the camp was gone, in its place, the military stride with which he was more familiar.

Within a few hours, Lieutenant Fitzgibbon had reached the British headquarters on the heights near Burlington and during a hastily arranged council of war he explained to his superior officers the condition of the U.S. camp at Stoney Creek. The information he had brought did little to brighten the faces of those gathered around the table. In fact they became even grimmer as Fitzgibbon leaned across the table, pointing out on the map the various positions of artillery, sentries, and supplies.

The U.S. camp at Stoney Creek was only a temporary stop-over. It sat on the edge of a low plain, a one to three mile wide belt which follows the western shoreline of Lake Ontario while butting the base of the Niagara Escarpment which rises sheer for an average of a hundred feet, then slopes gradually westward to Lake Erie. The Escarpment forms a natural barrier to any westward route and it stretches from the Niagara River to the shores of

They were bent on a plan to clear the Niagara Peninsula of the Union Jack.

the Georgian Bay like an immense wall of stone. Numerous creeks and rivers tumble and cascade down from its heights, yet there are few natural routes that give access to the land above. During a military operation a strong force on the heights could easily shut off a force twice its size on the plain below, even drive it into the lake. But the British had no such force; in fact they now stood on the verge of complete defeat. They were into the second year of the war with the U.S. and already the United States fleet under Chauncey had taken command of the Western end of Lake Ontario while Dearborne's army had thrust through the Niagara defences, had taken Fort Erie, Queenston Heights, Fort George, and then had stormed the northern shore of the lake at York and had sacked the small town and ravaged its fort. Now they were bent on a plan to clear the Niagara peninsula of the Union Jack and push north until they had established a new border that would slice away all territory west of a line running South from the Georgian Bay to Lake Ontario.

As the grim faced men sat watching Fitzgibbon's finger trace the perimeter of the U.S. camp on the dimly lit map, they knew the final British battle to hold Upper Canada was about to take place. On the lantern-lit map, his finger jabbed at the various strong points, places where most of the U.S. troops might be concentrated during an attack against the camp. The information was precise yet it did little to improve the British position. They were 700 Militia, Indians, and regulars against 1500 well-equipped troops. Already news had come that the U.S. was moving supplies and reinforcements down the lake

Their ammunition was down to 90 rounds.

while the British supply lines were cut and their ammunition now down to 90 rounds.

What came next jolted those seated around the table. For far from giving in to defeat, Fitzgibbon was determined to seek victory. He asked to be allowed to lead a night attack against the camp because he was certain that this would catch the enemy unprepared. Under his plan, the 49th would take the front line with the Indians, militia, and other regulars close behind. Since the attack he proposed would be made from the shallow ravine directly under the artillery positions, he also asked that all guns be unloaded and kept so until a few moments before the attack began.

Some thought that such an attack was not only preposterous, but downright lunacy! Even so, they were voted down and the decision for a night attack was made, and it gave Fitzgibbon the support he needed. The attack would be made the following night before the U.S. fleet could make contact with the camp. And though it might be the last blow for the British flag, at least it would be a defiant one.

Late the following afternoon Fitzgibbon led his men down from the heights followed by the other troops. As dusk fell, they were close to the American camp and they settled down in silence to await the coming night; by the light of the stars the first small group moved out. Their assignment was to silence the sentries while the rest of the force moved into position. Barely a sound came from the camp as Fitzgibbon moved his men into the shallow ravine and assigned them their positions directly beneath the artillery which sat already loaded and waiting. When all were ready, a signal was passed down the line to begin moving up to the top of the ravine. This had to be done with care for now each man's weapon was loaded and one accidental shot could bring disaster for the entire force. Then the second signal came; the whoops and screams of the Indians. Seconds later, the night was shattered by the thunder of muskets and the shouts of men. Dazed American troops rolled out of their blankets and made for the sound of the charge. They managed one volley from their muskets but already Fitzgibbon's force had swept over the artillery positions and they were now turning the American's guns on the startled U.S. troops. The American line broke as the first wave hit their ranks and they retreated from the camp carrying their panic to the troops in the rear. Those who broke free set the pace and nearly the whole of the camp fled for the shore of the lake, leaving behind their guns and supplies for the victors. By morning, U.S. Generals Chandler and Winder and 116 rank and file were prisoners. When Fitzgibbon saw that the American ships had arrived

Though it might be the last blow for the British flag, at least it would be a defiant one.

and were picking up the fleeing troops instead of supporting their land force he pressured his superiors to allow him to continue the attack on the fleeing Americans. But those in command were hesitant. They were already satisfied with their victory and it was another two days before the British force was moved up to 40-mile Creek, at what is now Grimsby, a bare 11 miles from the battle site at Stoney Creek.

Soon Fitzgibbon's impatience moved him to pressure his superior officers again, only this time he chose a different course. An American, Captain Chapin, with a band of 40-odd mounted men had been turned loose on the Niagara peninsula and they were marauding across the countryside, burning and pillaging the homes of the Canadian settlers. Although his barbarous acts had been condemned by Americans who demanded that he be stopped, the military refused to curb him. Chapin had to be stopped or at least countered, Fitzgibbon explained to his superiors, and then he offered to lead a small force of men which would carry a taste of their own medicine right through the American positions. Under his plan, a small force could move through the U.S. lines, then moving quickly from place to place they could wreak havoc on the supply lines and stores. On this he got agreement and a call went out for 50 volunteers to carry out the mission. The feeling for Fitzgibbon was so high among the troops that almost the entire regiment of the 49th begged to be accepted for the task.

Within days the green jackets, which had brought the 49th fame as the "Green Tigers", were replaced by red, and 50 grey jackets were added to be used to bring even more confusion to the enemy. Cow bells were taken along so that a code could be used to synchronize their movements when they were moving in small groups. Before long the special unit was working behind the American lines burning bridges, destroying supplies, and creating enough confusion to disrupt troop movements along the entire front. First they were here, then they were there. No one was sure who or what units were involved and by the time troops reached the area, the phantom unit had vanished. At one point, Fitzgibbon's force had Chapin's band cornered and they would have walked right into the trap that had been prepared for them. Instead, 150 American troops from Fort Erie blundered into the trap first.

Badly outnumbered, Fitzgibbon's small group melted into the forest leaving the Americans to mill around in their own confusion.

Later, at a small village further away, Fitzgibbon went into the village to see if there were any Americans about. He became involved in a fight with an American trooper and a Dragoon outside of a tavern. He had almost bested the two when the Dragoon broke free, grabbed a sword and was about to slash Fitzgibbon's neck. But as he raised the sword a woman came out of the tavern and wrestled it from his grip and saved Fitzgibbon's life. For this act of bravery the government later awarded her and her husband 400 acres of land, for it had allowed Fitzgibbon to live and carry on his guerrilla warfare against the American invaders.

The most defiant act pulled off by Fitzgibbon was in taking over the De Cou home in the middle of the American lines. From this base of operations he commanded the crossroads which led to Queenston Heights, St. Davids, St. Catherines, the Lake, and Colonel Bisshop's station—the post at Burlington Heights. The American lines of communication were severed, their movements practically at a standstill. Military headquarters at Washington was furious. The American juggernaut had bogged down and now British reinforcements were moving west while a crash program had been instituted at the Kingston ship building yards to give Yeo supremacy over the U.S. fleet on Lake Ontario before the fall. Orders were passed along to U.S. commanders to get Fitzgibbon and his band of guerillas even if it meant throwing the full force in to batter down the doors of the De Cou house. When the order came there were many willing to pass it on but few willing to carry it out. Finally the task fell to Colonel Boerstler. He was assigned 500 troops to do the job.

Colonel Boerstler asked that he be given until sundown to decide. Fitzgibbon gave him five minutes.

The point of assembly for this operation was Queenston, close to St. Davids, a little over 15 miles from the De Cou house. While troops were still arriving, two U.S. officers forced their way into the home of a wounded Canadian Militia officer, James Secord of the Lincoln Militia, crippled in the Battle of Queenston Heights. They demanded to be fed and while they waited for Secord's young wife to prepare food for them they discussed the coming battle against Fitzgibbon. The young woman, fearful of what would happen to the guerrilla hero of the frontier, went and told her husband. Confined to his bed, he could do nothing and he told her that she would have to make the trip through the brush to warn the Green Tigers. He told her to prepare the house to make it appear as though she had just stepped out to do some small chore, then she was to be on her way to De Cou's.

History records that this young woman succeeded in deceiving American sentries by using a cow as a decoy, then, bare-footed, she made her way through the dense bush. At Beaver Dams, a short distance from the De Cou house, she came on a band of Indians which had been brought up to assist the British troops, but none of these understood English. When the meaning of her message finally got through to them, they hussled her on to De Cou's where she told Fitzgibbon of the coming American attack.

There was no way the small force of 50 could stave off an attack by 500. Fitzgibbon ordered Secord's wife taken to safety, then he sent a rider to inform Colonel De Haren who was already on the road to De Cou's with a force of 200 British troops and Militia. During the early hours of the next morning Fitzgibbon heard shooting down the road near Beaver Dams and he took several of his men and went down the road to scout the area. When they arrived at the site they found that a force of two to three hundred Mohawks and Caughnawagas, a small band of which Secord's wife had stumbled onto, had moved in behind the American force and had cut off their retreat. The Americans had driven on to some high ground in a field at the side of the road. Fitzgibbon watched for a short time, but he realized that the Indian force hadn't the strength to keep the Americans isolated from the road back to Fort George. He also knew that it would take too long for his own men or those of Colonel De Haren to reach the scene.

Within minutes, fire from the Indian positions began to slacken. Fitzgibbon could wait no longer. He ordered one of his men to sound the cease fire and almost immediately the shooting stopped. Fitzgibbon was as amazed as the rest of his men. He grabbed a white handkerchief, fastened it to his sword, and marched directly out into the field. After a few moments the Americans sent one of their officers out to meet him. Fitzgibbon knew that the Indian attack along with their whoops and screams had unnerved the American troops. He boldly told the American officer that British troops had them surrounded and that their only retreat had been sealed by the Indian troops. Then he added that his superior officers were prepared to offer terms of surrender to prevent any further slaughter. If they refused, then the Indian force would be turned loose.

The American Colonel Boerstler was having none of it. He had seen nothing of a superior British force and demanded to be shown proof or he would resume the battle. Fitzgibbon replied that he would have to take it to his superiors and turned and walked from the field. Just as he was reaching the edge of the forest Captain Hall who had been scouting the area arrived with 20 of his men. Without waiting to explain, Fitzgibbon called him out into the field where he could be seen and told him to act the part of a superior officer.

The ruse came off and Fitzgibbon again returned to the field to inform the Americans of the refusal. When Colonel Boerstler asked that he be given until sundown to decide, Fitzgibbon gave him five minutes, stating that it would be impossible to hold the Indians at peace any longer than that. Boerstler finally accepted and terms of surrender were drawn up. Fitzgibbon had also discovered that among the American troops were Captain Chapin

and his raiders. Under the terms of surrender, Chapin and his men were to be sent back across the border on parole because it was believed that if they were held prisoner in Canada they would be murdered for their activities against civilians. Fitzgibbon agreed. He knew Chapin would receive worse treatment when they arrived back in the States.

But the battle was not yet won. For at this point Colonel De Haren arrived on the scene. He knew nothing about the American surrender. Fitzgibbon tried to keep him back while he explained that the Americans knew nothing of the small size of the British force. But De Haren continued to blunder right into the middle of it all. Fitzgibbon moved quickly ahead of him and gave the order for the American troops to move forward in single file. As they crossed the field, he tried to get De Haren to issue the command for the Americans to drop their arms before they could see how thinly spread the British troops were. When he received no satifactory reply, he asked if it was wise to let the Americans get so close to the Indian lines before they dropped their arms. At this point Colonel Boerstler blurted, "For God's sake, do as this officer asks." De Haren complied and Fitzgibbon passed the order to the Americans. Immediately the Indians swooped onto the field intent on collecting the weapons but the American troops, fearful of the Indians, were uncertain as to whether to drop their weapons or to defend themselves. Fitzgibbon sensed the tightness of the situation and he moved with the speed of a cat. In a moment he was on top of a boulder in front of the U.S. troops and in that instant made what has been called the shortest and most bombastic speech of his career. "Don't touch your weapons, Americans!" he shouted, "Not a hair of your head will be hurt! Remember, I am here!"

In the final tally, the total prisoners taken came to 25 officers, 519 non-commissioned officers and men, plus a 12-pounder, a 6-pounder, and two ammunition wagons.

Although the events at Stoney Creek and Beaver Dams stand out vividly in Lieutenant James Fitzgibbon's career, they are by no means the only ones in which his daring carried the day for the British. Before the War of 1812 finished, there were other battles and suffering before the British army, the Canadian Militia, and the Indians together retook the forts at either end of the Niagara River and re-established this natural line as the border between the United States and Canada.

For their service to the crown and to Canada, the 49th never received the reward or respect that was due them. When the war ended, they were in rags and tatters and most had nothing to cover their feet. Likewise the Indians and Militia were sent home empty-handed when they were no longer needed and most were left to themselves to reclaim what little they could of their past lives.

One glaring fact cannot be ignored: it is to Canada's everlasting shame that her country's youth find greater identity with the heroes of foreign lands than they find with those few such as Brant, Brock, and Fitzgibbon who carried the flame during Canada's struggle to nationhood.

sitting bull

Prophet or Pariah?

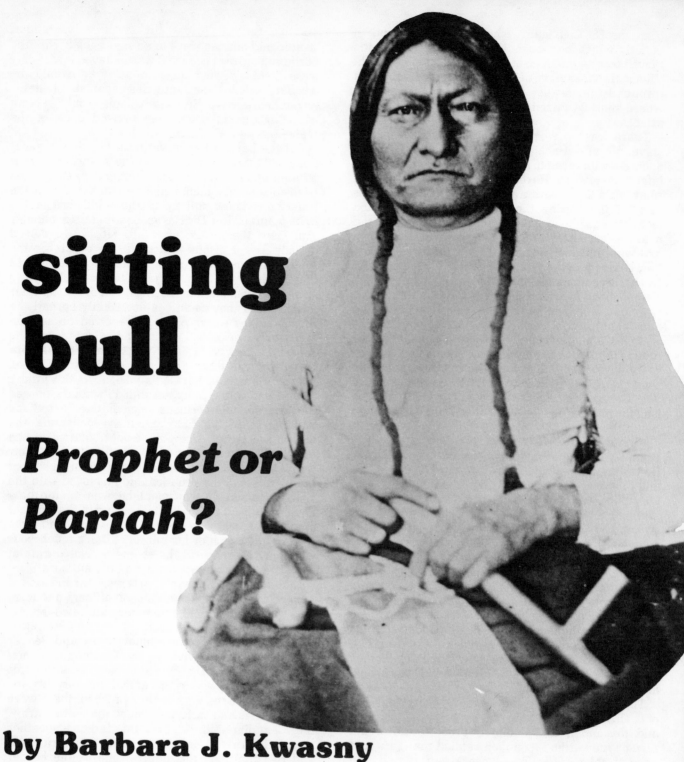

by Barbara J. Kwasny

"I read that they have buried his body like a dog's—without funeral rites, without tribal wail, with no solemn song or act. That is the deed of today...so let it stand for the present. But there is a generation coming that shall reverse this judgement of ours. Our children will build monuments to those whom we stoned."

So wrote 'Adirondack' Murray, American writer and former clergyman, when he learned of the circumstances of Chief Sitting Bull's death, in 1890. The last two sentences have a ring of prophesy.

In 1973, two Canadian books were published on the life of the controversial warrior. They are:

Sitting Bull, by Grant MacEwan, and *Across The Medicine Line*, by C. Frank Turner. As well, Andrew Suknaski has written and published the moving *Poem To Sitting Bull And His Son Crowfoot*, which appears in his collection *Wood Mountain Poems*. Sharon Pollock's play, *Walsh*, opened to enthusiastic audiences in Calgary, in the fall of 1973. It told the story of Major Walsh of the N.W.M.P., and his friendship with the exiled Sitting Bull.

This generation is building a monument of words and emotions to the much-maligned leader of the Sioux.

Sitting Bull was born about 1834, in what is now South Dakota. His father was Chief Jumping Bull of the Hunkpapa Teton Sioux, a warlike, aggressive, and proud people. At the age of ten, Sitting Bull distinguished himself as a brave hunter; by fourteen, he had become a warrior, and in his early twenties, he was becoming a respected influence within the band—their leader in peace and war.

In the plains Indian culture, fame and admiration could be won only through success in war and the theft of horses. Sitting Bull's "diary" of pictographs depict him as a fierce and brave warrior. The pictographs, which he drew, show him riding stolen horses, and dealing "Coups" to a total of sixty-three Indian and white enemies—all by the time he was thirty-six years old.

It is incredible that this brutal heritage of killing existed side-by-side with Victorian England, in a time when Gilbert and Sullivan were composing their light-hearted musical comedies; when Anna Karenina, War and Peace, Alice in Wonderland, and Around the World in Eighty Days were published; when Edison, Graham Bell, and Marconi were inventing their astonishing communication devices.

No wonder there was little understanding between whites and Indians in the west—here was a culture gap with a vengeance!

Sitting Bull resolutely refused to accept the influx of white settlers and prospectors into "his" Black Hills territory, and pledged to keep his lands, granted in the Treaty of 1868, for his own people, forever.

The Sioux revered him as a powerful medicine man, inspired spiritual leader, and a rather tyrannical chief who never wavered from his duty to lead and protect his "children." Americans, on the other hand, despised Sitting Bull as a murderous savage—leader of the 1866 Sioux raid on Fort Buford in the Dakota Territories, and villainous strategist of Custer's defeat at Little Big Horn in 1876. In their horror of Indian atrocities, they conveniently ignored the massacre of Indians by the army, the scalping of Indian women and children by whites.

Fear of retribution for the Custer massacre forced Sitting Bull to lead 4,000 of his Sioux "across the Medicine Line", to Wood Mountain, Canada, where they remained in exile for almost five years.

The first years in Canada were good. Game was plentiful; the Mounties' law stern, but fair. The Teton Sioux slept peacefully for the first time in the memory of many of the younger members of the tribe—out of reach of the American "long knives" and "blue coats."

At Wood Mountain, Sitting Bull formed a lasting friendship with Major Walsh, Commanding Officer of the N.W.M.P. post. He found, in the "Meejure," the first white man he could respect and trust.

Gradually, the buffalo were disappearing from the prairie, and since the "White mother" (Queen Victoria) would not grant these American Sioux reservation land to farm, by 1883, their plight was desperate. The Canadian government refused to supply provisions for the aliens, and the once-proud tribe was reduced to eating gophers and roots in order to survive.

Both the American and Canadian governments were determined that Sitting Bull and his followers would have to return to reservations in the U.S. The Americans demanded that on surrender, the Sioux must turn in their guns and horses, and forsake their hunting heritage.

In July 1884, Sitting Bull and two hundred faithful followers, who had refused to return to the States until their Chief could resign himself to reservation life, surrendered at Fort Buford, N. D. Eventually, starvation had succeeded where persuasion and diplomacy had failed.

The Hunkpapa Sioux were not allowed to return to their beloved Black Hills, but were resettled, first at Fort Randall, then at Standing Rock.

Sitting Bull accepted defeat fairly gracefully, and even consented to tour as an attraction with Buffalo Bill Cody's Wild West Show. The red men never won a battle in that Wild West, but Sitting Bull prospered in spite of his daily defeats. Cody was a benevolent employer, and saw to it that the chief lived in the best location, in the finest lodge, with the finest furniture, while on tour with the show.

When the season ended, the chief retired to his cabin at Standing Rock, with his cherished mementos of show business. Cody had given him a white sombrero, and a performing horse who had been trained to sit and raise one hoof, at the sound of gunshot.

Life was peaceful for several years, but in 1890, Sitting Bull was visited by Kicking Bear, a Minneconjou from the Cheyenne River Reserve. Kicking Bear brought news of the Ghost Dance, a frenzied marathon, in which many dancers fell to the ground, and while in a trance, saw the Indian Messiah. The Messiah promised that in the spring, new soil would bury all the white men, and the new land would be covered with streams and trees and sweet grass. The vanished buffalo and wild horses would return, and on this new earth, only Indians would live.

Word of the Messiah spread like a grass fire across the west, and in nearly every reservation, dancers in Ghost Shirts, painted with magic symbols to guarantee protection, were gyrating to the point of exhaustion, hoping to please the Messiah.

The agents, soldiers, and settlers were alarmed that Indians on far-flung reservations were united once again in the Ghost Dance. The agent at Standing Rock informed the government that the power behind the new religion was Sitting Bull, and recommended that the chief be arrested and confined in a military prison.

At daybreak on December 15, 1890, forty-three Indian police silently surrounded Sitting Bull's camp. Three miles away, the cavalry poised, ready to ride to the rescue in the best western tradition.

Sitting Bull was dragged from his cabin, and the ensuing uproar roused his warriors, who rushed to his aid. In the midst of the confusion, Buffalo Bill's show horse sat upright and raised his front hoof when he heard gunshots. Sitting Bull and his seventeen-year-old son, Crowfoot, were fatally shot, and only the cavalry's arrival saved the Indian police from annihilation.

One of Sitting Bull's prophesies to Walsh had been fulfilled. "If I return to the Americans, they will kill me."

* * *

Sitting Bull was buried in a wooden box, alongside white soldiers, in North Dakota. Years later, the whites' bodies were removed, and the chief was alone on the hillside, overlooking his hunting grounds. Over his grave was a simple wooden marker.

SITTING BULL
DIED DECEMBER 15, 1890

When this marker had been whittled away by souvenir-seekers, it was replaced by a cairn of stones, and later, by a cement slab, iron railing, and modest marble tombstone.

SITTING BULL
DIED
DECEMBER 15, 1890
CHIEF OF THE
HUNKPAPA
SIOUX

Later still, his bones were moved to Grand River, South Dakota, and reburied in an even more imposing tomb.

"Our children will build monuments to those whom we have stoned."

THE TESTIMONY

"He (Sitting Bull) resembled Gladstone—large-featured, thoughtfully grave, reflective, reposeful when unexcited... In conversation he was deliberate, the user of few words, but suave and low-voiced."

"Adirondack" Murray

"What treaty that the whites have kept has the red man broken? Not one. What treaty that the whites ever made with us red men have they kept? Not one. When I was a boy, the Sioux owned the world. The sun rose and set in their lands. They sent 10,000 horsemen to battle. Where are the warriors today? Who slew them? Where are our lands? Who owns them? What white man can say I ever stole his lands or a penny of his money? Yet they say I am a thief. What white woman, however lonely, was ever, when a captive, insulted by me? Yet they say I am a bad Indian. What white man has ever seen me drunk? Who has ever come to me hungry and gone unfed? Who has ever seen me beat my wives, or abuse my children? What law have I broken? Is it wrong for me to love my own? Is it wicked in me because my skin is red; because I am a Sioux; because I was born where my fathers lived; because I would die for my people and my country?"

Sitting Bull

"The only good Indian is a dead Indian."

General P.H. Sheridan—1869

SONGS OF SITTING BULL

"Young men, help me, do help me!
I love my country so;
That is why I am fighting."

* * *

"My father has given me this nation;
In protecting them I have a hard time."

* * *

"No chance for me to live;
Mother, you might as well mourn."

"Crafty, avaricious, mendacious and ambitious, Sitting Bull possessed all the faults of an Indian and none of the nobler attributes which have gone far to redeem some of his people from their deeds of guilt...."

James McLaughlin, agent Standing Rock

14

"We will yield to our neighbors—even our animal neighbors—the same right as we claim to inhabit the land. But we have now to deal with another breed of people. They were few and weak when our forefathers first met them and now they are many and greedy... This new population is like a river overflowing its banks and destroying all in its path. We cannot live the way of these people and we cannot live beside them. They have little respect for Nature and they offend our ideals.

Just seven years ago we signed a treaty by which the buffalo country was to be ours and unspoiled forever. Now they want it. They want the gold in it. Will we yield? They may kill me before I will give up the land that is my land."

Sitting Bull—before Little Big Horn

"The art of war among the white people is called strategy or tactics. When practiced by the Indian, it is called treachery."

General Nelson A. Miles

"This man, that so many look upon as a blood-thirsty villain, would make many members of the Christian faith ashamed of their doubts and weakness in the faith of their God. If they knew him in his true character—he was not a cruel man, he was kind of heart; he was not dishonest, he was truthful. He loved his people and was glad to give his hand in friendship to any man who believed he was not an enemy and was honest with him. But Bull experienced so much treachery that he did not know who to trust. How or by whom, you say, was he deceived? I would answer by saying everybody."

Major Walsh—N.W.M.P.

sitting bull
who dreamed about the possible
union of indians spanning the prairies
west to the shining mountains—
i wonder if his dream
floated as frosted helium before his eyes
the day the sun gleamed across the waiting guns
while men dragged him feetfirst from the tepee
like a dark sack of sins—

from Wood Mountain Poems—Andrew Suknaski

"The war between the U.S. and Bull was a strange one. A nation against one man. On the U.S. side there were numbers; on Bull's side there was principle. The one man was murdered by the nation to destroy the principle he advocated—that no man against his will should be forced to be a beggar. Bull was the marked man of his people."

Major Walsh—N.W.M.P.

"I am thrown away!"

Sitting Bull—on surrender at Fort Buford.

FIRST IN THE WEST

by Doreen Mierau

Fort Macleod police post and village in the 1880's.

On October 14, 1874, nine months after leaving Dufferin, Major James Macleod and his troop of Northwest Mounted Police began construction of Fort Macleod, the first police post in western Canada and home for the newly-formed NWMP Force.

Several weeks earlier, Macleod and his men had set out for the notorious Whoop-Up country via the Whoop-Up Trail from Fort Benton, Montana, with three objectives in mind: quell the illicit whiskey traffic in the lawless frontier region, establish good relations with the Blackfoot Indians and secure winter quarters for the exhausted men and horses.

No doubt the latter was foremost in Macleod's mind as they followed police scout Jerry Potts to Fort Whoop-Up on the site of present-day Lethbridge, Alberta. The sturdy, well-constructed fort appeared ideal for use as a police post. However, its sole occupant, trader Dave Ackers, rejected the Major's offer and Potts directed the column west to an island in the Old Man River where they lived in makeshift surroundings while building the new post.

The fort site was ideal. Excellent pasture and hay grew on the level bench on which the post was located. Ample wood for building and fuel was provided by cottonwoods that fringed the island. The high river banks offered shelter from the north wind; good water was plentiful as was wild game.

Situated thusly in the heart of Blackfoot country near the southern trading route to the United States, the post was to become headquarters for police activity in the troubled region.

Major Macleod and his men worked untiringly. The approaching winter and the burden of ailing horses, wrapped in blankets and sheltered in the bushes, (the healthy mounts were required for the return east with Commissioner French) caused the stables to be built first.

Stripped to the waist, the men cut and squared logs into 12-foot pickets. These were placed upright in three-foot-deep trenches to form the stockade which also served as the outer wall of the buildings. Living quarters for the officers and men, stables, work shops, stores, a hospital and a blacksmith shop were located facing inward in the 200-foot-square compound. Windows and doors were hauled by bull team from Fort Benton. The decision by the men to name the post after Commander Macleod was unanimous.

A sad note marred activities of the men during the construction of Fort Macleod. Thirteen days after arriving at the site Constable Godfrey Parks died of typhoid fever, after having been ill for some time. His body was the first to be buried in the little cemetery between the river and the fort. His death was the first for the "originals" of the force.

Macleod and his men set out for the notorious Whoop-up country.

By the first week of December, the Union Jack flew from the flagstaff and the men were settled, somewhat cramped, within the barracks; by the middle of the month the work was completed. And none too soon, for several days later the weather turned cold and four feet of snow covered the ground.

During the construction of Fort Macleod, the police made their first liquor arrest in the region. Ten men under Inspector Crozier were led to a sod hut at Pine Coulee, some 40 miles from the fort, by an Indian named Three Bulls, who complained that some traders had bartered several gallons of whiskey for two of his horses.

A colored man named Bond and four Americans were arrested. Two wagons containing cases of liquor, rifles and revolvers were confiscated as well as buffalo robes and sixteen horses. The liquor was

The liquor was poured out on the site.

poured out on the site. The prisoners were tried at Fort Macleod, the trial resulting in a fine of $200 each for Bond and two of the other men. The others, whom it was felt were less responsible for the crime, were each fined $50. The following day, a Fort Benton trader named Weatherwax arrived to pay all the fines except that of Bond. He was sentenced to jail but escaped while being transferred to another building at the fort.

Because many horses were required for patrols a "police farm" was established near the fort where the horses were wintered out. This method of maintaining a supply of fresh horses proved very helpful as the mounts were often ridden 50 miles a day for several weeks.

By the end of 1874 the NWMP had become well established in the west, having been divided into six detachments, the largest and most important of which was Fort Macleod with ten officers and 140 men.

Life for the police at the post was by no means the exciting one portrayed by newspapers in eastern Canada. The men were inexperienced and unfamiliar with the territory. In the event of an Indian attack, reinforcements were hundreds of miles away; communication with Ottawa existed only by telegraph via Fort Benton.

As well, trouble within the ranks was becoming evident. Forced to exist on a daily diet of tea, beans, flapjack, buffalo meat and rancid pork, many of the men showed their dissatisfaction by refusing to obey orders. The lack of replacement clothing was also evident. Many wore homemade caps and pants, blankets or buffalo coats. Raw buffalo skins were sometimes wrapped around boots to keep them together. What a motley crew they must have been on parade!

When the chinook—a phenomenon peculiar to the Fort Macleod region—arrived, the Mounties' work was softened somewhat, as was the mud on the roof of the hardly habitable barracks. Consisting of thin poles interwoven and covered with three inches of dirt, the flat roofs rained liquid mud on the contents of the rooms. Occasionally, a roof collapsed, creating havoc at the post. The cold, damp, earthen floors hardly promoted a healthy environment. Drafty walls and a wet and muddy blanket on a bed of ripped timber were not conducive to a good night's sleep either. In the bare dirt floor of the officers' mess the indentation of a buffalo trail was clearly visible!

Desertion from the ranks increased steadily. By the end of 1874, the men had not yet received their pay; 18 men had deserted to the Montana mines by

Desertion from the ranks increased steadily. By the end of 1874 the men had not yet received their pay. 18 men had deserted to Montana.

the time payroll arrangements had been made with a Helena Bank.

During March, 1881, 11 men deserted the force. The constant drills and parades, crowded living quarters, trivial duties and low pay were cited as reasons. Disgusted with their pay of 40¢ per day, when officers were receiving $1,000 annually, the constables resorted to near mutiny on several occasions. Fortunately, changes were made and conditions improved after petitions were presented to the Commanding Officers.

The addiction to alcohol was becoming noticeable among the men at Fort Macleod by 1880. Frustrated by the loneliness, isolation and lack of women in the western wilderness, many of the police turned to liquor as an escape. In 1884, four men were dismissed for drinking; in 1888 twelve cases of drunkenness were dealt with at the Fort. Punishment ranged from a $10 fine to three-to-six months in prison with hard labor.

The qualilty of the liquor available in the region left much to be desired. The poorest, selling at Fort Benton for several dollars a gallon, sold for $10 a bottle in the Fort Macleod barracks.

Unable to support the habit at such an expense, the men soon became adept at concocting their own substitutes. Jamaica ginger was a favorite, as was a mixture of raw alcohol and ginger extract that could be obtained for $1 a bottle. Occasionally, the men resorted to drinking red ink, Florida water and cologne.

Word of the situation reached Ottawa, and liquor permits were introduced stating that alcohol was permitted for medical use only. This step, though it failed to abolish the abuse of liquor, considerably suppressed the problem among the police.

Life in the barracks, however, was not without its humorous incidents. The fact that the police were composed of a cross-section of nationalities resulted in various clashes of personalities. The ranks of Fort Macleod were no exception; sons of European aristocracy were present there, as an incident

which occurred one morning behind the stables shows. A French count and a German baron were in the midst of a sabre duel with several Canadian-born constables acting as judges when they were discovered by an officer. No doubt, reprimands were handed out to all involved.

Constables at Fort Macleod devised various means by which to obtain confiscated drink. When a shipment of liquor was seized in the winter time, the constable noted where it was poured. Sometime later, he brought the resulting ice inside to thaw. When alcohol was disposed of during the summer, it was often poured onto the ground under which a container had been buried to catch the liquid.

Inevitably, settlement sprang up around the police post. Businesses followed, the first of which was the I.G. Baker Company, the Fort Benton firm which located their store beside the fort and was contracted to supply the police. T.C. Power and Brother, also a Fort Benton firm, carried on business there, as well.

Former whiskey traders settled around the fort to a legitimate way of life. One of these, Harry Taylor, owned the first hotel in Fort Macleod and one of the few in the Territories.

Clustered about the post were the sod shanties of the Metis and ox-drivers for the Bull Trail, the terminus of which was the fort.

The post was soon the centre of expanding trade. By 1875, a saw mill was in operation, a carpenter shop was opened and a blacksmith was carrying on a brisk trade. D. Horan established a boot shop; Alberta's first drug store was opened in Fort Macleod in 1884. Wood fires in the police barracks were replaced with coal which was obtained from Nick Sheridan, an old miner who opened the first coal seam nearby.

In 1878 the fort was improved. Shingles replaced the dirt roofs and boards were a welcome substitute for bare dirt floors.

Social life at the Fort Macleod barracks was usually obtained at the mens' personal expense. In 1876, they prepared a Christmas dinner for the

Respected and trusted by the Blackfoot for his fair dealing, Macleod was named "Stamixotakin," meaning "Bull's Head."

community. Included were the officers, settlers, traders and six prisoners from the guardroom. Beef, venison, buffalo roasts, plum pudding, butter at 75¢ a pound and eggs at $6 a dozen were served and paid for by the police.

Dances were held occasionally but the shortage of

C-troop, NWMP, at Fort Macleod, 1879.

unmarried women soon discouraged this pastime. Cricket, polo, rugby, baseball and tennis were some of the sports in which the police participated.

A business specializing in sweets and tobacco, with two billiard tables and poker tables, owned by an ex-whiskey trader Tony La Chappelle offered a welcome diversion to the police as well as the village residents.

Probably the best relations with the Indians were established at Fort Macleod. Respected and trusted by the Blackfoot for his fair dealing, Macleod was named "Stamixotakin," meaning "Bull's Head," feeling him to be as stalwart as the bull buffalo, the head of which was displayed in Macleod's office. Eventually, the symbol of the buffalo head, with the motto "maintain the right," became part of the police crest.

In 1877 Treaty Number Seven was signed at Blackfoot Crossing some distance from Fort Macleod, marking a significant milestone in police and Indian relations, as a result of fair dealing by the police at the post.

When the Sioux were making their presence felt on Canadian soil in 1876 two divisions of troops arrived from Fort Pelly. One was dispatched from Fort Macleod to establish Fort Walsh, the other remained at the fort. Three years later the number of men at Fort Macleod was reduced when headquarters were moved to Fort Walsh.

By 1881 Fort Macleod was one of two large

Alberta centres. That same year the fort was plagued with problems. Fire destroyed the quartermaster's stores and some stables. The course of the Old Man River changed, causing flooding which resulted in the current undermining the island on which the post was located. Several log houses slid into the water and were swept away.

A new police post was built in 1883 two-and-a-half miles south-west of the old site. One year later the buildings were occupied. Considered a masterpiece of building at that time, one million feet of lumber went into the construction of the post. The grey buildings were arranged in a 48-foot-long by 254-foot-wide rectangle.

In addition to the buildings contained in the former post, the new fort boasted a sergeants' mess and quarters, coal house, wagon shed, bakery, recreation and billiard room and an underground magazine covered with concrete and earth. As well, a large hospital was built which was said by Surgeon Kennedy to be the best in the Northwest.

Two 9-pound MLR guns and two mortars were the fort's defence.

The coming of the railway in 1892 brought an influx of settlers to the area. By 1901 the population of Fort Macleod stood at 796 and farming and ranching were becoming well established in the area.

Peaceful settlement brought about a decline in police activity at Fort Macleod. In 1919 it was reduced from a key divisional post to a detachment. When the entire force was reduced to 1200 men in 1922 the number of men at the fort was again decreased.

Today, 18 miles north of the largest Blood Indian reserve in Canada, a replica of the fort—with bastions and a catwalk—is situated on the north side of the town of Fort Macleod.

Inside, old photos, uniforms, weapons and Indian artifacts and regalia tell of an era when the cradle of the force was the bastion of law and order in Canada's west.

Commissioner J.E. Macleod, NWMP.

20

METIS TRIUMPH ON THE MISSOURI PLATEAU

by Hal G. Duncan

Near mid-June, 1851, a small party of Metis buffalo hunters left Grantown, Assinaboia, for the annual summer hunt.

Five weeks later, on the high slopes of the Missouri Plateau, they fought and won an incredible victory over an overwhelmingly large band of Sioux warriors. That victory ended for all time the threat of Sioux attack that had hung like an ominous shadow over the development and progress of the settlements along the Red and Assinaboine Rivers, in what is now the Province of Manitoba.

Since the first days of the Selkirk Settlers the Sioux had resented the settlements and the ever-widening intrusion of the buffalo hunters into territory they had ruled for many years, and had vowed to wipe out the white intruders and the Metis.

The ending of that threat by the Metis hunters was an important event in the settlement of the Canadian West that has been mostly ignored by historians. And it was a proud day in the history of the Metis people; one for which they received little credit in their struggle for recognition in the turbulent days of the Red River and North West Rebellions.

Metis buffalo hunts were the envy of their white counterparts. Well organized, they were conducted on almost military lines, with close supervision and discipline maintained by the captains of the hunt. Women were essential members of the hunt. They did the skinning of the animals, and the cutting and drying of the meat. Older children assisted with camp chores and gained first hand knowledge of the hunt.

The Grantown party was small—about 70 hunters, with women and children, and 200 carts. The party was led by Jean Baptiste Falcon, nephew of Cuthbert Grant the founder of Grantown, and accompanied by Father Louis Lafleche. Both Pierre Falcon and Father Lafleche were to play hero's roles in the days to come.

The threat of Sioux attack hung like an ominous shadow.

West of Pembina, Dakota Territory, the Grantown hunters made a prearranged rendezvous with parties from St. Boniface and Pembina. The St. Boniface and Pembina parties made a large camp—over 300 hunters, 1200 women and children, with 1000 carts for transporting the hides and meat. Rules and regulations were made for the hunt, and the combined camps started west. They were heading into Sioux country.

The hunt moved across the plains for many days. Even though no enemies had been sighted constant vigilance was maintained. The Sioux had long held sway over the plains over the Cree and Saulteaux tribes, and their traditional enmity for those two bloods was carried on to the Metis. The leaders of the hunt knew that trouble could be expected if

Sioux were encountered, but they were prepared to stand firm in their right to hunt the plains.

Small herds of buffalo were found, and runs made. The weather was favorable, and the meat and hides started to pile up in the carts. There was optimism that this was going to be a trouble-free hunt.

June had run out as the full party approached the plains between the headwaters of the Sheyenne River and the big bend of the Souris. At that point the Grantown party separated from the main body to hunt to the north. it was agreed that they would keep in touch with the main camp for mutual assistance if the Sioux should attack.

July 22nd saw the Grantown party arrive at the first uplifts of the Plateau. Riding on the initial escarpments of the Plateau five scouting hunters unexpectedly sighted a very large Sioux camp. They hurriedly signalled to the following hunters. Falcon immediately selected a sloping spot that offered some advantage in defence and ordered camp made.

Meanwhile the scouts had ridden into a hollow, but they were detected, and surrounded by fierce-visaged warriors. Guarded greetings were exchanged; then the hunters were asked to go to the Sioux camp.

Knowing they were actually being taken prisoners, two of the scouts broke away, with the Sioux in hot pursuit. Fearing hostilities, Falcon hastily prepared for battle. But the Sioux pulled up for parley, declaring that they had no warlike intentions, and that a small band would return the other scouts the next day, at which time they would expect some gifts of goodwill.

Falcon took this declaration with tongue-in-cheek, convinced that the Sioux would attack his small party, confident of victory. The two scouts vowed

Metis buffalo hunts were the envy of their white counterparts.

that there were almost a thousand warriors in the Sioux camp. Though it appeared hopeless to resist such overwhelming odds, Falcon felt flight was useless, and he ordered preparations made for a stand.

The carts were run into a circle, and the wheels barricaded with the meat drying racks, packs, saddles and hides. Trenches were dug beneath them for the protection of the women and children. At that point Falcon used a Metis tactic that was new to plains warfare; one which carried on to become famous in the downfall of the Metis at Batoche, in the North West Rebellion thirty-four years later.

Using the cart circled barricade to hold the oxen and horses Falcon moved his defense outside the barricade. A hundred yards or so out from the circle, each hunter dug an individual rifle pit from which to meet the expected attack. The hope was to keep the Sioux bullets and arrows away from the precious stock, and the women and children.

As dusk settled, two men were sent to find the main camp and bring help.

Sunday broke clear and warm. The camp was grim, and prepared for what might come. Father Lafleche celebrated Mass, and administered the sacrement to those desiring it.

Father Lafleche was kneeling in prayer when the Sioux appeared. It was not the small party, as promised, but the full fighting power of the band, awe inspiring in full war dress, sun glinting on headdresses, gun barrels and spears. Their hundreds of multicolored war ponies made a formidable front.

Each hunter dug an individual rifle pit from which to meet the expected attack.

A few hundred yards away the Sioux halted. Falcon, feeling they possibly weren't going to attack, sent hunters out to meet them and offer gifts.

The three prisoners were in the midst of the waving war bonnets and spears; sure that death was coming anyway, they broke away in a brave attempt to join their fellow hunters. On fast horses, two of them outdistanced the Sioux, but one, Malatiere, was overtaken and killed.

The killing of Malatiere showed the Sioux' intentions, and the hunters rode for camp, pursued by warriors, who rushed the circled Metis defence. The jockeying was over, and the battle that was to make Metis history was on.

Coolly and deliberately the hunters met the charge with a withering volley that killed the leading chief and sent several ponies and their riders crashing to the ground.

Nonplussed by the death of the chief and the deadly fire from the rifle pits, the Sioux went into the circling attack that had struck terror to the hearts of members of many wagon trains on the southern plains. But shooting from the protection of the pits, the hunters kept the circle from closing in. Warrior after warrior tumbled to the yellowing, dusty ground as the battle wore on.

Standing on a cart in the center of the circle Father Lafleche, dressed in his white surplice, encouraged and exhorted the Metis to stand firm. He carried a hatchet, which he was ready to use if the Sioux broke through. Falcon passed from pit to pit with ammunition and encouragement. Shooting from inside the barricade, Falcon's sister, Isabella, backed up the hunters with her rifle.

The sun reached the noonday sky as the Sioux attack faltered. Repulsed by the stout stand of the hunters, they withdrew to consult, giving the beleaguered defenders a brief respite. Then, gathering their pride as warriors, they rushed again in a thundering charge. But again, when within range of the pits, they circled, rather than face the losses a full charge would inflict. Again, the hunters held them off.

Weary of the long, losing battle, and sure that Father Lafleche, in his white robe, was a Manitou who protected the Metis from their bullets and arrows, the Sioux gathered their wounded and disappeared over a distant ridge.

The jubilant hunters rode out over the battlefield. Dead war ponies and Sioux lay sprawled on the

Metis buffalo hunters, 1873.

plain, and bloodstained patches of grass indicated many wounded. Malatiere's riddled body was found; the only Metis casualty besides a few horses and oxen.

Though victory was theirs, Falcon and his men were sure the Sioux would attack again when they regained their courage. After discussion, it was decided to try and join the main party. The two messengers who had left to alert the main camp had run into Sioux, and returned without accomplishing their mission.

Falcon posted sentinels, who kept a close watch through an anxious night, but there was no attack, though the throb of war drums could be heard throughout the night. By early morning preparations were completed and the retreat started.

Falcon again showed military ability in conducting the march. The carts travelled in four columns so placed that by one swinging left and one right a square could be quickly formed, and the barricades set up. Scouts rode out some distance on both sides and front and back.

The column had only been moving an hour when the rear scouts signalled the approach of the Sioux. The square was formed, with a double line of carts to give the precious stock more protection. The hunters ran out to dig their pits, while the women and children barricaded the carts.

Shooting from under and over the necks of their ponies, the Sioux again attacked in a whirling wheel of color and action. Again they were met by the Metis' bullets that sent ponies and riders crashing to their deaths. Again Falcon and Lafleche rallied the hunters in their desperate stand in the heat, dust and smoke. The roar of gunfire mingled with the wild warcries of the attackers. But still the Indians couldn't whip themselves into facing the Metis bullets in the head-on charge that would have surely brought them victory.

The killing of Malatiere showed the Sioux' intention.

The battle raged for several hours before the circling slackened and the warcries died away. A chief rode in with an arm raised in the upturned palm sign of peace. He was told to stay back or he would die. He replied that the Sioux had had enough, they were leaving and would never bother the Metis again.

Unbelieving, the hunters crouched low in their pits as the whole war party circled the pits and fired a tremendous volley of bullets and arrows in a last grandiose gesture of bitter defiance before vanishing over the rim of the Plateau.

Buffalo hunters camp on the western plains.

Father Louis Lafleche.

The hunters ran in from the pits. Their total casualties were three wounded. Not a horse or an oxen had been killed, nor a woman or child hurt. Led by Father Lafleche the whole camp knelt in thankful prayer.

It was learned later that in the two day battle, upwards of eighty Sioux warriors had been killed, as many wounded, and over one hundred ponies killed. It was a humiliating defeat for the 'tigers of the plains', one from which they never recovered. True to the chief's declaration, never again did they raid or threaten to raid the land to the north, or the settlements on the Red and Assinaboine rivers.

Won by bravery and unequalled fighting hardiness, and strategy, the victory did much to achieve prestige for the Metis in their efforts to establish themselves as a race of people.

That glory and prestige ended at Batoche, North West Territories, in 1885. There the Metis had risen in rebellion against white dominance and settlement of the prairie land which threatened their way of life. Their faith in the invincibility of the rifle pits was destroyed when troops of the Canadian Militia overran the pits at Batoche to defeat the rebels.

The defeat at Batoche ended any recognition the Metis had received as a race through their gallant stand on the Missouri Plateau, but proud memory of the victory and its contribution to the settlement of the Canadian West still lives.

FREDERICK DALLY
Pioneer Photographer

by Joan Bellinger

The camera clicks, there is a pause, and the picture is fully developed before your eyes, in color. Quite a change from the days when photography took hours to process, the equipment was heavy and cumbersome, and travelling with it was a real chore. This was the task faced by Frederick Dally, pioneer photographer, who labored with his equipment over the tortuous trails of the Cariboo, to the gold strikes at Barkerville.

Frederick Dally was born in Wellingborough,

Quamichan Indian Village—Vancouver Island.

"Ne'r-Do-Well" Dump—Grouse Creek, in the Cariboo.

Northamptonshire, England, around 1840, and educated at the famous Blue Coat School in Christchurch, London. In 1862 he emigrated to B. C., landing at Esquimalt, from the China-clipper Cyclone, four and a half months after he left home. Trained as a portrait photographer, he soon opened a studio in Victoria, at Fort and Government Streets, where he spent about eight years. His pictures of Victoria and Vancouver Island have gone down in history.

Dally had a great time photographing a glassy-eyed group who were having a great deal of trouble sitting still.

During his eight years in Victoria, Dally made numerous forays into the then "wilds" with his camera and equipment.

It was in the summer of 1867 that many of his adventures began, when he accompanied Governor Seymour and party into the Cariboo to photograph the creeks and general terrain. All sorts of exciting things happened.

Some of the exuberant miners decided to give Seymour a 21 gun salute, which was a great idea, but between each blast of the nitroglycerine, the Governor and his staff were fortified with a glass of champagne. By the time 21 rounds had been fired, Dally had a great time photographing a glassy-eyed group who were having a great deal of trouble sitting still.

While in Barkerville, the photographer established a studio, making perhaps more money than some of the miners.

Dally enjoyed the scenic setting of the gold rush town, and the brilliant stars and northern lights, the like of which he had never seen before.

On a late-night excursion, he noticed, as well as the northern lights, the sparks coming from the many chimneys down below—the saloons and dance halls—and he wondered if they could start a fire. When he mentioned this possibility around Barkerville, he was assured the lumber from which the buildings were constructed, would never burn. On that very afternoon, the conflagration which literally destroyed the town began.

At the back of Barry and Adler's saloon, a dance hall girl was spurning the ardent attentions of a miner because, it seems, she was trying to iron a dress. During the struggle, a stove pipe was loosened and the flames caught the canvas ceiling. The fire spread so rapidly, nobody had time to douse them, but instead, the townsfolk dashed around collecting their clothes and effects. Dally had no time to set up his darkroom tent, or sensitize a negative, so the excitement went unrecorded.

He was there the next day, though, equipment at the ready, to photograph the sad scene of devastation; the plight of homeless survivors.

Photography in those days was a real chore and only the truly dedicated attempted it. As well, only relaxed subjects could be taken, as the people had to stay in one position for a full six to eight minutes. Nothing instant about that, or the fact that the photographer had to do his developing at the scene, using a dark tent.

He was assured the lumber from which the buildings were constructed would never burn. On that very afternoon...

In this dark tent Dally also made the negative, flowing a collodion mixture over a glass plate, dunked in silver nitrate. This was then drained and put in a plate holder, and later put in the camera with the hope that it would work.

After the picture was taken, it was back to the tent for partial development, and later, varnishing.

In the home darkroom, on fine notepaper, washed in solutions and dried in the dark, prints were made. This was known as the 'wet plate' process, in use around 1880, and the amount of gear required was overwhelming. Buckets, tubs, trays, and bottles, a bed of cotton batting in a tin tub to keep the various jars and vials from breaking, a rack to hold the glass plates, plus a whole barrel of water. Imagine this equipment being packed over gold rush trails, along with a thirty pound camera—a big black box in two sections, one sliding inside the other. The front end had the lens, while the back had the ground glass for focusing. This was accomplished by pulling the rear of the camera backward.

Cameras in those days did not have a diaphragm to open or close, and there was no shutter, but you capped the lens with a round cardboard box lined with velvet. When photographing, you took off the cap, counted the many minutes on your watch, and replaced the cap. Dally had a wagon to haul the barrel of water, and sometimes erected his tent on it.

In addition to all the hazards of photography, Dally was contending with frequent bad weather, summer heat, dust, wind, flies and those huge Cariboo mosquitos. Once, while attempting some picture taking on the bluffs of Pavilion Mountain, he was attacked by eagles. No wonder he ended up taking a course in dentistry.

Fortunately, Dally kept excellent records and made numerous notes to go with his pictures. He had many adventures, as well, on his trip around Vancouver Island, when he took pictures at Nootka

Gold mining rocker at Williams Lake, in the Cariboo.

of some tattooed Indians, many of the men quite naked. It is likely that he took the first pictures of Indians in Quatsino Sound, and at a seashore Indian village near Comox he noted a smoke smudge at the end of the beach from the burning corpse of a girl who had died of some disease.

Dally was a young man and the hardships of travel did not daunt him for he journeyed over many forest trails to take pictures of the Cowichan River fish trap and Father Rondeault's hilltop stone church, and an Indian village at Quamichan Lake.

It was near the old stone church that he found a pile of human skulls, evidently left over from some long ago tribal battle. When the photographer picked one up to look at it closely, a large snake darted its head at him out of an eye socket. The snake must have been more frightened than Dally for he later picked up the same skull and sent it back to London where it is in the Museum of the Royal College of Surgeons.

Whether Dally tired of all this adventure is not recorded, but he sold his business in Victoria to Messrs. Green Brothers in September, 1870, and was listed amongst the passengers on the 'Pelican' bound for San Francisco, in October, 1870.

In a letter to his sister Emma he announced his acceptance at the Philadelphia College of Dentistry where he commenced studies in 1870 and graduated in 1872. At least he wouldn't have as much equipment to pack around. ⊕

These photographs were taken by Dally the day BEFORE and the day AFTER the disastrous Barkerville fire in September of 1868.

WINTERING ON HUDSON BAY

by Ken Webb

"Lagopus lagopus" could very well be a mournful cry for the dead, and well it might have been had several hundred men known this Latin name for the willow ptarmigan of northern Canada. This large bird, which turns white in winter to match its surroundings, is very plentiful along the shores of Hudson Bay and James Bay. To the crews of four seventeenth century European expeditions to these same shores, lagopus lagopus was either a symbol of nature's bounty or a ghostly apparition just beyond reach.

The first of these four was the infamous last voyage of Henry Hudson. Arriving at the southern end of James Bay in the autumn of 1610, the famous navigator and his crew of 21 found themselves desperately low on food with an unknown winter about to set in. With the help of a large catch of lagopus lagopus, and the bud of a tree which we'll see about later on, these first Europeans (since Viking days) to winter in the Canadian Arctic survived til spring, though just barely.

The first sign of scurvy is a loosening and blackening of the teeth.

In 1612, Thomas Button became the first Englishman to winter in Hudson Bay proper, at the mouth of the Nelson River in present-day Manitoba. He arrived better prepared with staples for 18 months, but whereas dried and salted staples may prevent outright hunger, they lack essential vitamin C. The losses from scurvy on this expedition would surely have been greater again without the fortunate appearance of large numbers of lagopus lagopus. The meat of most animals contains vitamin C, and the willow ptarmigan was by far the most numerous game these explorers encountered.

The voyage of the Dane, Jens Munk, in 1619 - 1620, was much less fortunate. Scurvy hit these 65 men so hard that even when lagopus lagopus strutted past their ships anchored near present-day Churchill, Manitoba, no one had the strength to catch their supper. As the first sign of scurvy is a loosening and blackening of the teeth, neither would they have had the ability to eat much of this white bird had they caught any. In the case of Munk and his two fellow survivors of that terrible winter, the saviours were roots, sprouting plants and berries in spring. These they mercilessly hunted down on all fours.

Twelve years later, Thomas James led the last of these early voyages in search of a northwest passage through Hudson Strait. He arrived at Charleton Island in James Bay with 21 men in the autumn of 1631. Despite having no shot to kill the odd groups of lagopus lagopus which offered relief from rampant scurvy, they managed to escape in the spring with only four deaths. Again, they seem to have relied more on the curative powers of early spring plants.

For all four expeditions, winter was a double-edged sword. Not only was the sub-Arctic winter miserably cold, but it also prevented them from escaping until the ice broke up in the spring. They of course had no control over its length and severity, and could only wait for it to end. What they did have control over was the way they adapted to winter. But expecting a milder European-type winter, their preparations were inadequate to say the least.

They were generally lucky in choosing favourable wintering sites with some degree of natural protection against the ship-crushing ice. James, for instance, just happened to winter in what has been called the safest place in the southern part of James Bay, used in later years by Hudson Bay Company ships.

They all had reasonably wind-proof shelters. While Button and Munk wintered on board their ships, Hudson and James had their men build wooden shelters on shore. In the case of James, it was lucky they had housing on shore as the ship had

The life-saving *Lagopus lagopus* [willow ptarmigan] in winter.

to be abandoned over the winter. Their three buildings, two for living in and one for storage, were constructed of logs piled six feet deep.

Winter clothes were inadequate on all four expeditions which isn't surprising when you consider what they were used to. January mean daily air temperatures must have been between -20° and -30° C with an added wind-chill factor off the Bay. Munk, who had lived in Norway, was probably the best prepared. In October he distributed shirts, shoes and boots to his crew.

In the middle of winter some of James' crew found themselves with no shoes, having scorched them in the fire in a vain attempt to warm up. Nonetheless, they were forced to carry on with their hunting and wood gathering in makeshift footwear. Meanwhile, hoar frost covered their bed-clothes, their sleeping area being just out of reach of the central fire.

Fire was their greatest weapon against the cold of winter, but keeping one going when wood was so difficult to obtain meant constant work for all able-bodied men. In all four cases there were trees growing at no great distance. But James' crew found they couldn't use green wood as it smoked too much. Dry wood smoked only slightly less and

made them "all look as if we have been free of the Company of Chimney-Sweepers." They relied on dry standing trees, as fallen ones were covered by the deep snow. To add to their troubles, hatchets had a way of breaking in the cold air.

The sub-Arctic winter prevented them from escaping until the ice broke up in the spring.

As long as they were healthy, Munk had his men out collecting wood and burning it for charcoal. By April, however, scurvy had so decimated them, that they were reduced to burning pieces of the ships. Part of the heat generated had to go into melting snow for water. Meanwhile the beer and wine they had brought had frozen solid; they had to be boiled before they were drinkable.

James had the same problem when, in December, all liquids, including sacke (a dry wine), vinegar, and oil froze "as hard as a piece of wood, and we must cut it with a hatchet." They had dug a well in November, the water in the ponds below the ice being undrinkable. In December the well froze up.

They later found a spring which produced a constant flow of fresh water for the duration of the winter.

The cold also limited hunting. The snowfall along the western shore of Hudson Bay is quite heavy, making hunting and wood gathering difficult chores. Jens Munk lamented his not having brought snowshoes of the type used in Norway. Henry Hudson offered rewards for fresh meat to those who would brave the cold and deep snow. In later winter, several men went out with Thomas James after a deer, but returned with nothing but large blisters which laid them up for two weeks.

The weakening effect of scurvy, and ever threatening outright hunger in the case of Hudson's crew, also reduced the amount of hunting and wood-gathering possible. As the only way of preventing scurvy was to have a regular supply of fresh meat or vegetables, a vicious cycle began.

The Hudson Bay lowlands, which includes the

The three buildings were constructed of logs piled six feet deep.

wintering sites of all four expeditions, is tundra-like along most of the immediate coastline. Vegetation here is generally low to better resist the cold winds off the Bay. Just inland, however, patches of conifers gradually appear, and it was in this mixed zone, between the tundra and boreal forest, that Hudson, Button, Munk and James sought refuge.

In the autumn, when they arrived, they were able

A typical view from any of the four wintering sites described.

to gather berries. Munk appears to have had the best luck with these, perhaps because many of the same plants grew in Scandinavia. Munk noted in his journal that the several men with him who were suffering from scurvy after the long sea voyage recovered quickly with the help of these whortle-berries, cloudberries, gooseberries, and crow-berries. Unfortunately, the bushes were covered with snow during the winter.

When spring finally arrived there were still some berries remaining on the bushes. But the three survivors at Munk's haven found it easier to nibble on the fresh green shoots just pushing up from the ground, as the first step in their recovery.

Scurvy had so decimated them, that they were reduced to burning pieces of the ship.

James' men were able to start gathering sprouting vetches on the last day of May. Boiled and fed to the sick, they had an almost immediate positive effect. By June 9, those men who had been bedridden with scurvy, were up and walking around. During the remainder of their stay, boiled vetches, vetch juice, and raw vetches on bread formed a major part of everyone's diet.

In July, James found a scurvy-grass growing along the beach, which proved better (in taste?) than the vetches. After setting their captain afloat, twenty years before, Hudson's men had been reduced to eating a type of grass, having used up all the food brought with them.

Now comes an interesting question: why were there so many deaths, especially on Munk's expedition, when even in winter fresh vegetation was available. There were, of course, no fresh greens as we think of them, and the berry bushes lay beneath the snow, but there were coniferous (evergreen) trees. Within easy reach of all four expeditions were spruce, juniper, and/or pine, all of which retain needles throughout the winter which are high in vitamin C.

In the autumn, they were able to gather berries.

Henry Hudson's was the only one of these four expeditions which made any use of trees in the fight against scurvy. One day during the winter, Thomas Woodhouse returned with buds from an unspecified tree. These were boiled, and the resulting tea given to "them that were troubled with ache in any part of their bodies." Prickett (who wrote the official report in lieu of the dead Hudson) goes on to say that "for my part I confess, I received great and present ease of my paine."

This wasn't the first time Europeans in Canada had used part of a tree to cure scurvy. In 1525, Jacques Cartier and his crew, wintering near Quebec City, had also suffered from scurvy. Cartier finally asked the Indians of the area how they prevented the disease. With their advice, he prepared a drink of boiled bark which did the trick.

Captain Thomas James.

Unfortunately for them, neither Button, Munk nor James encountered any Indians. One Indian did visit Hudson's camp in the spring, but was unable or unwilling to help them with food. James went so far in his search for natives as to start a forest fire, in hopes that it would attract someone's attention. The fire got out of hand, and almost burned him alive.

The story linking scurvy and trees is a continuing one in Canadian history. The lesson that the needles, buds and bark of Canadian trees were readily available to prevent scurvy, never quite became common knowledge. As late as the 1890's men needlessly withered away in the Klondike while all around them were trees.

Meanwhile, back in the seventeenth century, we find that both James and Munk came close to this discovery. In his journal James relates that "there was no tree, bud, nor herbe but we made tryall of

Hudson's men had been reduced to eating a type of grass.

it." But instead of drinking the concoction, the men would twice daily immerse themselves in it. These herbal baths did soothe their aches temporarily, but how much more permanent would their relief have been had they only taken a drink of the stuff.

Munk also found that herbal baths helped. His were made by throwing in all sorts of herbs from the surgeon's chest. As the names were given in Latin, Munk was never quite sure what the baths contained.

The original map of Munk's Winter Harbour; present-day Churchill, Manitoba.

Sir Thomas Button.

With known edible plants so scarce during the long winter, Hudson, Button, Munk and James directed most of their fresh-food expeditions against the animal kingdom. In the spring, Hudson's and Button's men were able to catch fish. A few deer, some trapped foxes, a polar bear and a few other miscellaneous mammals were the only land game any of them took.

Birds, however, were generally plentiful. Despite the large number of water fowl that invariably turned up in the spring, few were killed due either to lack of shot or strength to pull the trigger. This brings us back to the willow ptarmigan, lagopus lagopus, one of the few birds adapted to Arctic and sub-Arctic winters.

Button reports killing over 1800 dozen birds, mostly "white partridges" as the English called the ptarmigan. Hudson's men killed some 100 dozen, while Munk and James were considerably less fortunate. Munk's men were too weak from scurvy to kill those which were around, while James' men were frustrated with a lack of shot.

Wintering on Hudson Bay—definitely dangerous business in the 17th Century.

SAMUEL ZIMMERMAN

From Prosperity to Tragedy

by Pauline A. Pottelberg

The first decades of the 19th century in Canada were marred by depression, wars, rebellions and financial troubles. Outlying settlements were scattered along the Great Lakes and the only link between them was by lake and river or across country through wilderness.

By the 1850's, however, prosperity had come to Canada. And one of the symbols of this new and marvellous prosperity was the construction of the railways which linked the scattered settlements together.

The first railroads in the world were built in England in the 17th century. They consisted of horse-drawn wagons on wooden rails and were used to haul coal and iron. In the 18th century when inventors in England, the United States and France were experimenting with steam locomotives, iron rails were introduced. James Watt, the Scottish inventor, had patented a steam engine as early as 1769, and in 1801 Richard Trevithick, an English engineer (1771-1833), invented a steam locomotive capable of pulling a heavy load.

The first locomotive to run on an American railroad was the *Stourbridge Lion*, imported from England. More were to follow, and by 1830, cities along the Atlantic seaboard became the nerve centres of many railroads. Inland points were quickly connected, and the success of the railways soon undermined the value of the canal and the turnpike.

It was natural that these inventions should become known and used in Canada. In 1834, the legislature of Upper Canada granted a charter to build a railroad of single or double track with wooden or iron rails between London and Burlington Bay, and to the navigable waters of the Thames River and Lake Huron. No action was taken.

Samuel Zimmerman, a young American in his twenties, emigrated from Pennsylvania to Canada in 1842. Although penniless, he was a man of enterprising nature and soon allied himself with men of wealth and convinced them of the advantage of a canal which would join Lake Erie and Lake Ontario.

Thus Zimmerman obtained the contract to build the Welland Canal and this gave him his start toward his spiralling empire. He soon became one of the most influential men in Canada: he built canals, bridges and railways. He became a banker, shipowner, railway contractor and millionaire. He owned real estate in Hamilton, Toronto and Niagara Falls. But he is best remembered for his connection with the railroads.

Zimmerman was a man of enterprising nature, and soon allied himself with men of wealth.

The charter granted in 1834 was about to lapse when it was amended and renewed in 1845. The amendment allowed the company to construct a railroad from any point on the Niagara River to the Detroit River, and the name of the company was to be "Great Western Railway Company."

The proposed route was to extend from Windsor, Ontario, to the Suspension Bridge at Niagara Falls via Chatham, London, Woodstock and Hamilton. The town of Brantford, although included in the original plans, was bypassed because civic officials refused a monetary grant to the railway company.

In October, 1849, the first ground was finally broken at London, Ontario. The Great Western Railway was no exception to the fact that construction in those days was done mainly by hand with pick, shovel and wheelbarrow. Oxen were used for hauling.

Marshes, seemingly bottomless, had to be filled

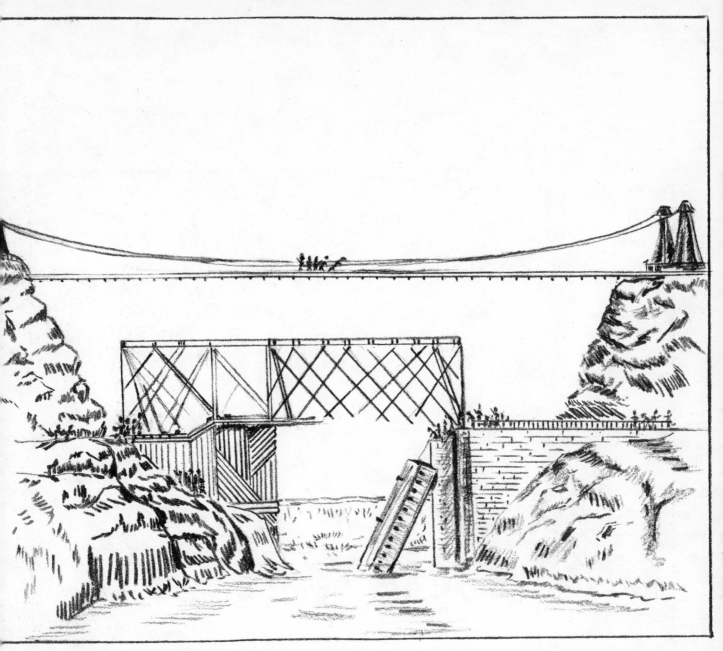

Scene of the Great Train Disaster at Desjardins Canal near Hamilton, Ontario, March 12, 1857.

and levelled. Bridges had to be built where it was difficult to find solid footings for the abutments. All grading and track-laying was done by hand. However, the building of the railway proceeded quickly, despite the enormous engineering problems encountered.

Nevertheless, the public was dissatisfied with its progress and insisted upon opening the railway almost before the tracks were well-settled. Thus in November, 1853 the first part of the line was opened between Niagara Falls and Hamilton.

By the end of 1856, most of the Great Western Railway had been completed and the company owned more than seventy engines, many of them passenger locomotives.

Samuel Zimmerman's next business venture was to be the construction of the Great Southern Railway. Then came that fateful day, March 12, 1857.

The Great Western Express between Hamilton and Toronto had been in operation for only a year and was already a popular mode of travel.

It was a bleak, cold day in Toronto and the shoppers waiting at the station to return to Hamilton

The road beds were improperly laid, the rails were of poor quality.

were anxious to gain the warmth and comfort of the train that would take them home. Among those waiting was Samuel Zimmerman.

Whether Zimmerman knew the real extent of the shoddy quality of his railways or whether he trusted to Lady Luck is not known. The roadbeds were improperly laid, the rails were of poor quality and the axles of the cars were not hardened to the extreme cold of our winters.

First locomotive used in Ontario [1852].

Although the passengers read reports of railroad accidents happening recently, they were comfortable and happy in the warm car.

The train was forced to slow to a crawl at the approach to the trestle bridge high over the Desjardins Canal near Hamilton. A freight train derailment here earlier had left a rough track. As he eased his locomotive onto the sixty-foot high bridge, the engineer felt it begin to give. Before he could stop his train, the bridge gave way completely and the train plunged into the canal, striking the ice with tremendous force. Over sixty of those on board lost their lives. Samuel Zimmerman was one of them.

This was Canada's first great train disaster and it had its effect on rail traffic. (See Canadian Frontier-Vol.4, No. 2 for a complete account of the Desjardins Canal accident.)

Although there were reports in the press that the accident was the result of poor material and

The bridge gave way and the train plunged into the canal, striking the ice with a tremendous force.

Early Railway Station—Great Western.

workmanship in the building of the bridge, the jury at the inquest blamed a broken axle.

When the railway decided to repair the bridge instead of rebuilding it, the public outcry forced an examination of all railway companies and scandals were soon given the light of day. Many cabinet ministers who were also directors of railway companies were suspect of wrongdoing. And it was many years before the railway removed the afflicted car from the canal so it was generally believed the verdict of the broken axle had been wrong.

Be that as it may, it appears that progress was rushed at the expense of many lives.

A poor harvest followed the train disaster and the large revenues anticipated by the railways for the transportation of goods to market were not realized. The combination of scandals, resulting in decreased use of railroad facilities, together with the poor harvest, threw Canada into another depression.

As Zimmerman went, so went his empire. His bank folded and disappeared by 1861, and his luxury ship, the *S.S. Zimmerman*, burned two years later.

The railroad which had brought Samuel Zimmerman fame and fortune so quickly just as quickly took it away.

THE *TALLAHASSEE*
A Fighting Ship
by Eugene L. Hamm

Halifax, Kipling's "Warden of the North", has seen the men and machines of many wars come and go. The fighting ships of many nations have sought haven within, and have sailed to glory from her rock bound harbour.

Not the least of these sea warriors was the "Tallahassee", that armed merchant cruiser of the

Washington had sent 13 ships on a search and destroy mission, with the "Tallahassee" as the objective.

Confederate States, during the Civil War in America.

Christened "Atlanta", at her launching in England, this ship was designed specifically to run goods through the Union blockade of Confederate ports. An iron, twin screw steamer, 200 feet long, she presented a low profile at sea, with a hull

moulded to offer the minimum of resistance in moving through the water. Her 700 horsepower engines gave her an outstanding speed for the times: 14 knots.

The "Atlanta" was bought by the Confederate government and brought to Wilmington, on the Cape Fear River in North Carolina. She was renamed "Tallahassee" and fitted out as an armed merchant cruiser against the ships of the Union merchant fleet.

On August 4, 1864, the Tallahassee left Wilmington, under the command of Captain John Taylor Wood, with orders to intercept Union shipping along the Atlantic coast. As it was impossible to bring prizes to Confederate ports, the ships were to be sunk.

Steaming down river, the Tallahassee was engaged by Union navy ships in the estuary but with superior speed, escaped—without damage—to the open sea.

During the next 12 days, Captain Wood put his ship among the Union merchantmen, like a wolf in a flock of sheep. Thirty ships, carrying precious cargoes for a warring nation, were sent slipping down through the cold grey waters of the North Atlantic. At the end of this period, with coal running low, Captain Wood laid course for Halifax to bunker.

The Tallahassee arrived at the harbour mouth in a flurry of flying spray, scrambling for the safety of neutral waters, with two Union warships hot on her trail. Washington, having heard of her exploits, had sent no less than 13 ships of war on a search and destroy mission, with the Tallahassee as the objective!

Now came the game of naval chess: England being a neutral country at the time, Union ships could not engage the Tallahassee in Canadian waters. By the same rules, the Tallahassee could not remain in Halifax harbour longer than 48 hours.

What was Captain Wood to do? The Union ships, Huron and Nanesmond, were the navy's fastest, and gave him little chance of escape. Being a resourceful man, Captain Wood applied for an extra 24 hours, ostensibly to do repairs on his ship. Despite

At one place, there was less than four inches between the ship's keel and the channel bottom.

pressure from Union sympathizers, the Admiral in charge of the Halifax station granted this extension.

The Tallahassee was taken to Woodside (now Mobil) wharf, for coaling and repairs. Captain Wood set off immediately to find a pilot. He was directed to Jock Fleming as the best in the business,

and subsequently engaged Jock to guide them out of the harbor by way of the Eastern Passage.

The Eastern Passage from Halifax harbour is a shallow, twisting channel lying to the east of McNab's Island, giving access to the Atlantic, east of the main harbour entrance.

There was, at that time, approximately 6 feet of water at the most shallow point of the channel, during low tide. Tallahassee drew 13 feet with coal and guns aboard.

Jock Fleming, however, was an old hand at the piloting game in Halifax harbor. With a high tide at midnight Jock thought there would be water enough to float the Tallahassee. But how could they get her length around the sharp turns of the channel? Captain Wood said, "Jock you find the water, I'll use alternate propellers as thrusters to swing her stern."

Shortly before midnight, several officers of the Royal Navy, who had been visiting aboard, bid Captain Wood "Godspeed" and returned to their ships. Quietly, the Tallahassee slipped away from the wharf. With Jock Fleming calling directions, Captain Wood put his ship through the darkness of a moonless night, into the treacherous Eastern Passage. With engines turning slowly and every member of the crew keyed to a high pitch, she inched along. At several places, Jock Fleming had a man in a row boat ahead, sounding the channel. At one place, by the lead, there was less than four inches between the ship's keel and the channel bottom!

After what seemed an endless time, the anxious mariners saw Devil's Island light ahead. Soon they felt the welcome, mighty power of the North Atlantic lift their ship, setting her free from the grip of shallow inland waters.

With a booming farewell and a wave of his hand, Jock Fleming was over the side to his boat and home—another job well done.

Captain Wood ordered a full head of steam. Soon the Tallahassee's mighty engines were throbbing in the night.

Dawn saw the Tallahassee far over the horizon, on her way to fresh adventures. The Union hounds of war awoke to find their quarry flown.

When the Civil War ended, Captain Wood—a rebel still—returned to Halifax to make his home, living out his days as a valued member of the community.

Jock Fleming always regarded his night trip through Eastern Passage as the highlite of his career.

Charles Wood, Captain Wood's son, grew to manhood in Halifax. He graduated from Royal Military College at Kingston, Ontario. Later he fell; the first Canadian officer to die in the Boer War. His son, Zachary Taylor Wood, a great, great grandson of President Zachary Taylor, of the United States, joined the Royal Canadian Mounted Police, rising through the ranks to become a commissioner. Left to remind us of these bold men and stirring days is Tallahassee Public School, on the eastern fringes of Halifax harbor.

The "Tallahassee"

THE AGONIZING DEATH
OF THE
DUKE OF RICHMOND

by Vera Fidler

Charles Lennox, 4th Duke of Richmond, Governor-in-Chief
of Canada, 1818-19.

A few miles south of the City of Ottawa a unique stone monument stands beside the road: unique because it is the only monument in Canada erected to the memory of a person who died of hydrophobia (rabies). He was Charles Lennox, the 4th Duke of Richmond who, on August 28, 1819, after suffering "unimaginable tortures," died in a nearby settler's house. He had been infected, when bitten by a pet fox some two months before.

At the time of his death, the Duke was Governor-in-Chief of Canada and was on an inspection tour of a number of military settlements in Upper Canada (Ontario). He had welcomed the appointment as Governor-in-Chief the year before for, although he had behind him a distinguished military and political career in Britain, he was heavily in debt, a situation he hoped to remedy in a new country.

He gained much notoriety by fighting a duel with his Colonel.

Born in 1764, Lennox joined the British Army at an early age. He was always a colorful figure: when he was twenty-five and in command of a company of the Coldstream Guards, he gained much notoriety by fighting a duel with his Colonel, the Duke of York, second son of King George III. The reason for the duel, from which both emerged unscathed, appears to be lost in the mists of time. In a second duel with a noted pamphleteer who had libelled him, the Duke seriously wounded his opponent.

He was a member of the House of Commons for sixteen years and on the death of his uncle became a member of the House of Lords. In 1807 he was appointed Lord Lieutenant of Ireland, a position he held for six years. In Ireland his lavish entertaining and extravagant spending made him very popular but also put him deep in debt. In 1813, as a means of retrenchment, he joined the staff of the Duke of Wellington in Brussels and took an active part in the Waterloo campaign. There, his wife made history by giving a glittering ball on the eve of the Battle of Waterloo. During the ball, word was received of Napoleon's plans to march on Brussels, but even as Wellington's officers hurried away to take up their battle stations, the dancing went on.

The Duke arrived at Quebec on July 20, 1818 and immediately became immersed in his duties. One of his main interests was the formation and progress of several military settlements of disbanded soldiers in Upper Canada planned "as a safe communication (route) remote from the frontier and defensible in time of war."

Soon after his arrival he made a tour of some of the settlements and in the summer of 1819 decided to make a second and more extensive tour through the Western districts. Accordingly, accompanied by Colonel Francis Cockburn, Deputy Quarter-Master-General, Colonel George Bowles, the Duke's Military Secretary, his personal servant, a man named Baptiste, and a number of soldiers, he set out in late June. He also took with him his pet dog, a bull terrier called Blucher.

Leaving Quebec, the party travelled up the St. Lawrence River to Fort William Henry (now Sorel, Que.). There, as he was about to inspect the garrison, he stopped to rescue his dog from an attack by a pet fox running loose in the courtyard. In a flash the fox seized his hand, sinking its teeth to the bone. The wound bled so profusely the other members of the party advised the Duke to discontinue the trip, but he laughed off any thought that it might be serious and refused to change his plans.

From Fort William Henry the party travelled as far west as Drummond Island, the most distant post at the northern end of Lake Huron. On the return journey, toward the end of August, they stopped at Kingston, on Lake Ontario, where they were royally entertained. From there they travelled on horseback north to the Perth settlement where they were again entertained and where the Duke became very irritable and complained of feeling feverish. Cockburn and Bowles tried to persuade him to take the road to Brockville from where he could return by boat to Montreal. But he insisted on going on to Richmond, founded on the Jock River the year before and named in his honor.

Setting out in the early morning of August 24th, the party had gone only a short distance when the Duke suddenly leaped off his horse and began walking. Full of feverish energy and unmindful of swamps, bush and windfallen timber, he walked some fifteen miles to a store where they were to stop for the night. There, according to Cockburn's record of the trip, the Duke spent an almost sleepless night "....and only joined us for a short time at breakfast, left us suddenly and went up to lie down until we were ready to start about eight o'clock."

He stopped to rescue his dog from an attack by a pet fox.

Now the trail was impassable for horses and the whole party set out on foot. But after six miles the Duke became so exhausted they had to stop at a settler's shanty. At this point they were met by Colonel George T. Burke, superintendent of the Richmond settlement, who had come to escort them to the village, and it was decided to arrange for the Duke to make another overnight stop, this time at the house of a Sergeant Vaughan. Accordingly, Cockburn and Burke went ahead "for preparing Vaughan's house and making arrangements in Richmond previous to the Duke's arrival," leaving to Major Bowles, the Duke's secretary, the task of getting him to Vaughan's later in the day.

Early the next morning Cockburn sent a basket "with some refreshment" from Richmond to Vaughan's and a note warning of the swamp they had passed through and suggesting that the Duke "not attempt the fatigue of passing (through) it." In answer, the Duke replied that he had difficulty in swallowing but would be in Richmond rather early. Cockburn did not expect him until about noon "but to my surprise about ten I was informed he was entering the town. I immediately went out to meet him." Shocked by his dishevelled appearance, his clothes wet and dirty and "looking particularly ill," Cockburn asked the Duke if he would not go to the tavern where he was to stay and change his clothes.

But his irritated reply was that he would rather see what was to be seen first.

Finally, "with considerable difficulty," Cockburn and Bowles got him into the tavern where he spent most of the day resting. He did visit the superintendent's quarters and became posted on settlement affairs, but he refused to inspect anything within sight of the river.

"I cannot relish my wine as usual...if I were a dog I should be shot as a mad one."

At the banquet held that night in his honor, showing no signs of fatigue, he was in high good humor throughout. But afterwards, as he and Cockburn sat sipping wine before retiring, the Duke suddenly pushed his drink away. "I don't know how it is, Cockburn," he exclaimed, "but I cannot relish my wine tonight as usual and I feel that if I were a dog I should be shot as a mad one."

Later that night, Mrs. Hill, wife of the tavern owner, heard him pacing the floor. He called for Bowles, his secretary and she heard them talking and afterwards described how the whimpering of the Duke's dog, Blucher, gave her a sense of impending tragedy.

By morning, the Duke was too ill to eat or drink. When Baptiste, his servant, brought a basin of water to his room, he could not bear to even wet the towel and even after Baptiste wet it and placed it on the dressing table, he had to "rub his face hard before he could prevail on himself to raise the towel to it." And when, after refusing breakfast, he tried to drink some tea he "became convulsed at which he was much annoyed..."

Only then was it realized that his symptoms could mean only one thing—Hydrophobia. Those with him sent for Dr. Christopher Collis, surgeon of the Richmond settlement, who had started for Richmond Landing on the Ottawa River where the Duke's party were to board a batteau for Montreal. Meantime, because the Jock River was navigable as far as a farm owned by one Chapman, three miles downstream, and because the road was so rough, it was decided that the Duke, with Bowles and Baptiste, should travel that far by canoe. There Cockburn and Burke would meet them with horses for the ride to Richmond Landing.

After much persuasion, the Duke agreed to this plan and managed to walk to the river. But the sight of the running water brought on such a severe spasm that hope of getting him into the canoe was almost abandoned. Finally he rallied and shouting, "Charles Lennox was never afraid of anything!" staggered into the canoe. The effort brought on another spasm and as the men paddled down the river, he seized Baptiste by the throat and demanded that they return to shore. As soon as they touched land, the Duke leaped out and with the others in pursuit, ran at top speed through the woods toward Chapman's farm. There, seeing Cockburn and Bowles who had just arrived, he jumped over a rail fence and ran into the barn where he collapsed. The men followed him in and laid him on some bundles of corn.

Toward evening they managed to get him into Chapman's log house and when Surgeon Collis arrived, he bled him "with little or no relief." However, between paroxyms of pain he became quite calm and dictated a letter to his daughter,

The sight of the running water brought on a severe spasm.

Mary, which Bowles took down to deliver personally to her in Montreal. In the letter he sent messages to his family and friends: "Tell March (his son, the Earl of March)...that I am satisfied I leave my titles and estates to one of the most honorable men in England...Tell my mother I know she possesses the soul and spirit of a Roman matron...She will rejoice her son died in honor although he did not have his wish of doing so on the field of battle...Tell my sister, Emily Berkley, to set a good example to my family who will need it...Give my love to the Duchess (his wife) and tell her to remember me to the Regent (Prince of Wales) and the Duke of York (his opponent in the duel)...Remember me to Angelsea and Jane Paget and the Duke of Wellington...Let my funeral be moderate in the Lower Province on the ramparts of Quebec...Tell Sarah that with my latest breath I forgive her and General Maitland (they were his daughter and her husband, Peregrine Maitland, who had eloped when the Duke refused to consent to their marriage. He apparently had forgotten that a happy reconciliation had taken place and when he came to Canada as Governor General he brought Maitland with him to be Lieutenant-Governor of Upper Canada, a post he held for ten years)...I die in charity with all the world and in perfect confidence of mercy from the Almighty..."

The Anglican Cathedral, Quebec, where the Duke was buried in a vault. From a water color by Mrs. M.M. Chapin.

Soon after dictating the letter his condition became worse. Complaining that he felt cold all over, he was seized with fits of uncontrollable shivering. At eight o'clock in the evening of August 28, 1819 he died lying on the floor.

The next day his body was placed on a mattress suspended on four stakes on a wagon box and taken by ox team over the eighteen miles of rough road to the Ottawa River and from there by canoe to Montreal and by steamer to Quebec. On arrival there on September 2nd, the body lay in state until the 4th when it was taken to the Anglican Cathedral. A long procession of military and government officials and ordinary citizens followed the hearse to the church. The body was interred in a Cathedral vault between the pulpit and communion table where today visitors can see the plaque marking his grave.

On August 17, 1926 a large crowd gathered at the old Chapman farm (now called Twin Elm Farm) for the unveiling of the stone monument erected by the Historic sites and Monuments Board of the federal government in memory of Charles Lennox, the 4th Duke of Richmond, who died there 107 years before.

CANADA'S FIRST PLAY

by Janet Craig-James

Canada's first play was presented 370 years ago under the most unusual circumstances. The stage was the sea. The backdrop, the rugged hills of Acadia. And the lighting was provided by the shimmering Indian summer sun in the sky above New France.

It was in the Autumn of 1606—November 14, to be exact—when Sieur Jean Poutrincourt, explorer, adventurer, and second governor of Acadia, stood on the deck of his two-masted barque which had just struck anchor in the Basin off Port Royal.

Poutrincourt was startled by the thunder of cannon coming from the fortress.

A touch of frost had transformed the trees on the mainland, turning the hills to red and gold as they sloped gently towards the water's edge. But Poutrincourt saw none of this. He was deeply troubled and depressed. He was returning from an unproductive exploration trip down the coast as far as Cape Cod and had accomplished nothing which would add lustre to the French crown.

Something else was adding to his worries. He had been gone for a number of months, leaving his friend, Marc Lescarbot, in charge of the Habitation. The Habitation had been established in 1605 by Sieur de Monts, who was its founder and first governor. Samuel de Champlain had chosen the site and drawn up the plans. It was merely a group of buildings arranged around a courtyard, fortified at

THE FIRST PLAY IN CANADA, 1606

C.W.JEFFERYS

the two southerly corners by the cannon platform and a stockade.

While Lescarbot was a fine soldier, he was, more than anything, a poet: a dreamer. One who envisaged the culture of France being brought to this wild, new land. But the men at the fort were a mixed lot. Voyageurs, soldiers, and half-civilized savages of the Micmac tribe. These were men of action who needed and demanded excitement and activity, of which there was none at the Habitation.

There emerged from the waves at the bow of the barque, King Neptune, Monarch of the Sea.

And so Poutrincourt wondered how his friend had fared with them. Would Lescarbot have succeeded in keeping them occupied and happy, or would they have deserted or even worse, mutinied?

As the crew prepared the shallops (small boats) for the trip to the mainland, Poutrincourt strained his eyes towards the shore. Even as he did so, as if in answer to his unspoken questions, he was startled by the thunder of cannon coming from the perimeter of the fortress, followed by the blaring of trumpets from within the pallisades beyond.

As Poutrincourt stared in amazement, there emerged from the waves at the bow of the barque, King Neptune, Monarch of the Sea, complete with white, flowing beard, golden crown and blue robe. He was being borne along on a cunningly disguised Micmac float, pushed by six monstrous Tritons as attendants. Behind these came four canoes, each paddled by a brilliantly painted naked Micmac warrior, bearing a gift.

Poutrincourt realized that this was some kind of welcoming ceremony planned in his honour, and instantly his gay, Gallic temperament responded to the spirit of the occasion. He recognized in this greeting the touch of his friend, Lescarbot, and knew he had him to thank for this water masque or play which was about to unfold.

Stepping into his impromptu role in this dramatic presentation, the Governor drew his sword, as if on the defensive, and waited for the performance to proceed.

King Neptune addressed him in verse, referring to him by the Indian name 'Sagamo', and reminded the enthralled Poutrincourt of his (Neptune's) great power to either help or destroy soldiers and explorers of all nations. He assured the Governor, however, that he would be his ally in all undertakings.

At the end of this part of the performance, and having been assured of Neptune's goodwill, Poutrincourt sheathed his sword, and was then addressed by four of the Tritons, who, speaking in unison, pledged their allegiance to the Governor and the French in their endeavours.

The fifth Triton delivered his speech in Gascon, while the sixth wished long life for Henry of Navarre, King of France.

At this point in the play, Neptune's float made way for the canoes manned by the Micmacs, bearing gifts for the Governor. The first gift was a quarter of moose; the second: beaver pelts; the third: belts and bracelets made of wampum; and the fourth: a harpoon. Having acknowledged the gifts, Poutrincourt knelt before Neptune and thanked him for his promise of aid.

This, apparently, ended the first portion of the play. Poutrincourt, by this time in high spirits, replied warmly, praising those who had taken part in the masque, and inviting everyone to the Fort to break bread. At the climax of this speech, the sound of gunfire and trumpets from the Fort sent long, rolling echoes resounding through the hills on shore.

Now, the Governor and his men entered the small boats, and, joining the flotilla, were rowed to the beach.

As he approached the gate of the Habitation, Poutrincourt saw that laurel twigs had been fashioned into crowns by the men of the Fort, and these now encircled the arms of France which had been set above the entrance. Over this was inscribed the motto of Henry V, 'Due Portegit': One Protects Two. Beneath this was the armorial ensigns of de Monts, with the Motto, "God Will Give An End Even To These Labours', and that of Poutrincourt, which means, 'To Valor, No Road is Easy.'

Once again the Governor was greeted with verse, this time by a merry fellow standing by, who finished off the play by addressing a group within the gates of the Habitation, urging them to 'fall to' and heartily enjoy the feast which was spread for them.

Had the play been presented on a conventional stage, the curtain would then have fallen.

Lescarbot wrote and rehearsed the first play performed by what became known as the Neptune Theatre.

Thus it was, thanks to Marc Lescarbot, soldier, historian and poet, the first play in Canada was performed in the colony of what is now known as Nova Scotia. A tablet to his memory reads:

Praise God for Marc Lescarbot
Who living hereabouts 1606-07
Wrote and Produced Nearby
America's first play.

Lescarbot, had, indeed, found a way to bring pleasure, mental stimulation and peace of spirit to his compatriots, huddled in the Habitation on the bleak shores of Acadia, just eighteen months after the establishment of the colony there.

During Poutrincourt's absence, in order to keep the men at the Fort occupied and oblivious to their harsh surroundings, he wrote and rehearsed the first play performed by what became known as the Neptune Theatre. A program of the play was entered in Lescarbot's 'History of New France.'

To honour Lescarbot and his successful efforts to bring culture to the New World, the Neptune professional repertory theatre has been established in Halifax, N.S. This, it is hoped, will be a permanent tribute to the one, who, over 370 years ago was responsible for what we might even now consider 'experimental' theatre.

The call of the West! One hundred and sixty acres of fertile land free! That is—almost free; ten dollars filing fee, a contract to build some sort of a dwelling and stick it out on the land for at least six months of every year for three years. Also the homesteader had to bring fifteen acres under cultivation. On a quarter more suited to ranching, the settler could prove up by fencing in eighty acres and keeping twenty or so horses or cattle.

With the completion of the Calgary-Edmonton Railroad in 1892, hundreds of homesteaders, single and with families, flocked into the area surrounding, for miles out, Siding 16, which is now the small city of Wetaskiwin.

In the glowing accounts, nothing was told of the vastness of the wilderness land.

In those glowing accounts encouraging settlers to follow the railroads West, nothing was told of the vastness of this wilderness land, the lack of roads or even trails, and even worse, the lack of communication with the outside world. This loneliness was broken only by the arrival of the mail with the occasional letter from home, sweetheart or friend and perhaps a newspaper. Many were the heroic, faithful carriers of Her Majesty's Mail. They braved mudholes and snowbanks, treacherous river crossings and slippery hills to deliver those precious bags of mail to pioneer post offices. These post offices were usually located in settlers homes and other settlers came perhaps once a week to pick up their mail and discuss the latest local news with the post mistress. Pay was so small that it was usually the wife's task to sort the mail and hand it out to callers as they came.

This writer's father, grandfather and grandmother homesteaded across the Battle River, east and south of Wetaskiwin, in 1893. Their first post office was located at the Lewis home just east of the river. It became known as the Lewisville Post Office.

Modes of travel suited conditions... whatever the day called for, the mail had to get through.

To reach the Lewisville office, the mail carrier, a Mr. Joe Cowan, usually ran a real obstacle course both summer and winter. Beside various creeks and axle-deep mud holes in the spring and summer, the Todd Crossing of the Battle River posed many a problem, especially in the spring when the ice broke up and water levels were high. Joe Cowan's modes of travel suited conditions; saddle and packhorse, two wheeled cart and packhorse and when the load was heavy and mud deep, a covered wagon and four horses. Whatever the day called for, the mail had to get through.

In late fall when ice started to form, water in both creeks and rivers was usually low, but the ice was not heavy enough to hold up the horses and sometimes had to be broken up before the horses were driven through the icy water. When the ice became firm, horses had to be shod sharply.

HER MAJESTY'S MAIL OF THE 1890's

by Huldah B. Franklin

Sometimes sand or straw was strewn across the ice before the snow fell.

In winter, the mail was usually carried in a covered sleigh. There were days when heavy winds piled the loose snow into deep snow banks, obliterating the trail. In open country, a new trail around these places could overcome this difficulty but many times horses had to be plunged through the deep snow forming a road on top of the drifts. This type of road became higher and higher as the winter progressed and in the spring thaw, when the snow became soft, horses plunged through and had a hard time making progress. Sometimes a way had to be opened with a shovel. Yes, the stalwart pioneers and their mail driver had their problems both summer and winter, but they seemed to expect these difficulties and headed into them without obvious complaint.

From Lewisville, Mr. Cowan headed north-east to Duhamel, a French Metis settlement twenty or so miles away on the same winding Battle River. Following the old Red River Cart Trail, he soon encountered the chain of lakes that ran through a valley for about twenty-five miles. Here the trail crossed the chain on the sandy bottom of a neck joining two of the lakes. This crossing was sometimes hub deep and widened into a bullrush bog. But Cowan usually made it, and detouring here and there where the settlers' fences barred the road, he slowly progressed to Duhamel where he delivered another lot of mail.

Settlers in the area received mail once a week.

Crossing the river again, he headed north-west and wound his way over and through this hilly country to leave his last lot of mail at Rosenroll, later renamed Bittern Lake.

The following day he returned to Wetaskiwin over the same route, picking up outgoing mail along the way. So settlers in this area received mail once a week. Mr. Cowan held this job until 1906, when a railroad was built from Wetaskiwin east through Camrose and on to Hardisty. This railroad serviced much of his territory.

Well does this writer remember our mail days. Rain, shine or a snowy 50 below, Dad went the five miles to pick up our mail on Saturday afternoon or evening. In addition to the expected letters and Wetaskiwin paper, we received regularly several weeklies: the Family Herald and Weekly Star, the Western Home monthly and others. Great was the excitement when the mail arrived!

On Sundays, when morning chores were done and dinner over, we'd all sit down to enjoy the papers. First mother read aloud our pages, then we youngsters would quietly amuse ourselves as she read The Quiet Hour in The Family Herald, the only religious service we knew.

Yes, much credit is due our early mail carriers who, though poorly paid, seldom failed to bring us our weekly joys regardless of rain, sleet, snow or prairie mud.

ECHOES OF A DISTANT WAR

by Hugh A. Halliday

Newspapers concentrated on the exploits of British generals.

For more than twenty years, from 1792 to 1815, England was locked in warfare with Revolutionary and Napoleonic France. Understandably, Canadian newspapers carried detailed accounts of the military and naval actions which were fought in distant places. The war affected British North America as well, most notably by spurring the timber industry as Britain sought alternatives to Baltic timber, denied the Royal Navy through Napoleon's continental blockade. The papers of the day did not comment extensively upon this aspect; economics was as dismal a topic in 1806 as in 1976.

There were other effects. Many Canadians joined the British forces, including four de Salaberry brothers, three of whom would die overseas in the service of the British army. Some joined the Royal Navy. Charles Rollette would serve at the Battle of Copenhagen; later he would have a distinguished career both ashore and afloat in the Great Lakes during the War of 1812. Again, however, the work of these men was little noticed at the time. The newspapers concentrated on the exploits of British

generals. They had little space for Canadian seamen and staff officers.

Nevertheless, the distant war did produce echoes in local papers and in ways that could be seen by the ordinary man in the street. One was in the manner by which ships came and departed. Although French naval power had been crushed in such actions as Cape St. Vincent and Trafalgar, privateers and small warships continued to menace shipping between Britain and North America. The British responded by adopting the convoy system, with groups of merchantmen being herded across the ocean under the protection of Royal Navy warships. Thus, in its issue of May 22, 1809, the Quebec *Mercury* announced that convoys from Quebec to the United Kingdom would sail about June 10, July 10, August 10, September 10, October 28, and November 15.

Not all ships joined these convoys; merchantmen were normally armed in any case, and many captains were willing to take their chances alone on the high seas. This was especially so with ships sailing to Quebec, for it was well known that most privateers operated either in the eastern Atlantic or in the West Indies.

On May 15, 1811 the brig *Fortune* sailed triumphantly into Quebec, carrying a general cargo and three passengers, including Alexander Greig of that city. The ship was badly shot about, her spars and rigging damaged and her sails riddled. The *Fortune*, mounting eight cannon and two swivel guns, had beaten off a French privateer of sixteen guns. In manpower the enemy had had the advantage of 120 to 19. The epic story was recounted by the Quebec *Mercury*:

The ship was badly shot about, her spars and rigging damaged and her sails riddled.

"The *Fortune* was attacked on the 13th of April, in about 53 degrees North Latitude and 20 degrees West longitude (Author's Note: south of Iceland). The action lasted for an hour and twenty minutes. On coming in sight of the *Fortune* she hoisted English colours, and on approaching hailed, and desired Captain Hodgson to send his boat on board; which he refused, saying that if they had any business with him they might send their boat to him. Whereupon the stranger immediately hoisted French colours, and fired a shot between the *Fortune's* masts, and then gave them a broadside, which was immediately returned by two broadsides. The enemy made three attempts to board. In the first attempt they poured in men in all directions, eight of whom got into the *Fortune's* jolly boat, at her stern, when one of the crew, with great presence of mind, drew his knife and cut the fastenings of the boat, which precipitated them into the sea. Numbers having gained the forecastle, Captain Hodgson ordered a discharge of musketry and then charged them with the bayonets. Those of the boarders who were not killed on the deck were thrust from the shrouds and chains into the sea.

"During the engagement the *Fortune's* colours were twice shot away, and were at last nailed to the gaff by a young boy who, while in the act of so doing, became a mark for the enemy; but he, far from being intimidated, called out to them, 'fire away, you b---rs'... She would probably have been captured, had she not fortunately shot away the enemy's fore-topmast, at which time the *Fortune's* crew gave three cheers, and the privateer sheered off. Captain Hodgson gave her

a parting broadside, which was not returned."

In the battle the *Fortune* had sustained three men killed and five wounded. The passengers themselves had taken part in the fighting; Greig, the Quebec citizen, had been hit in one knee. On the other side it was estimated that between 20 and 30 Frenchmen had been shot or drowned during the boarding attempts. No guess was made as to how many had been killed aboard their own ship.

As a mark of respect, the captains of those ships present in Quebec held a banquet in the old Union Hotel, with Captain Hodgson (whose given names the paper resolutely failed to divulge) as guest of honour. A contributor to the *Mercury* also penned a verse which expressed the pride of the citizenry, although it showed no great talent on the part of the poet:

"The Frenchman sail'd out, strong in men, guns and shot. Hard knocks his intent 'gainst rich cargoes to barter; 'Voila la Fortune; mines of gold are my lot.' But ah, sad reverse! Monsieur caught a Tartar."

The Stranger immediately hoisted French colours and fired a shot between the Fortune's masts.

Another aspect of the war was Royal Naval recruiting, which was, simply stated, legal kidnapping by press gangs. Not unnaturally, the press gangs preferred to pick up experienced sailors rather than hapless landlubbers, and any merchant ship that appeared to be over-manned was fair game for the navy. This was the background to an incident involving the merchantman *Anthorne* and the warship HMS *Thalia*, reported in the Quebec *Mercury* on May 15, 1809:

"Yesterday, as the *Anthorne* was coming into the harbour, the crew, seven in number, observing the *Thalia's* boat on her way to board them, immediately took the ship's boat, for the purpose of saving themselves from being impressed. In their hurry they lowered one end of the boat before the other, by which means all the seven fell overboard. Four were unhappily drowned; the three others were saved by the *Thalia's* boat."

In North America, far from the battlefields, the Napoleonic Wars still claimed their victims, unwitting and unwilling participants in a distant conflict.

THE BATTLE OF FISH CREEK

by
Victor Carl Friesen

Gabriel Dumont, Riel's military leader.

When Gabriel Dumont and his Metis buffalo hunters pushed west from Manitoba's Red River country to take up winter quarters and eventually permanent holdings along the South Saskatchewan River in the 1860's, their new abode was known as the St. Laurent settlement. This community stretched some thirty miles along the river, consisting of small huts, smeared with clay, and finer two-storey homes of squared logs, with neatly mortised joints at each corner.

One can easily imagine stampeding herds of buffalo pummelling over the edge.

Today, the place-name "St. Laurent" pertains to a ferry crossing east of Duck Lake and to a nearby log church, which, painted silver, gleams brightly in the morning sun from its site on the west bank. Close at hand, a sign directs to a "Buffalo Pit" within walking distance. Standing on the lip of a huge ravine which leads to the river, the viewer looks down on the tops of towering spruce trees. He can easily imagine stampeding herds of buffalo pummelling over the edge, bawling in terror as the animals in the rear, harried by the Metis hunters, pushed those in front to their death. Such a scene has been painted by several western artists.

Yet it is not this ravine which has the greatest claim to fame in the old St. Laurent settlement. To see the second ravine, one must cross the river and travel south along a winding trail on the opposite bank. One must go past Batoche, six miles away and the headquarters of Louis Riel in the North-West Rebellion of 1885; past Gabriel's Bridge, six miles

51

farther south where Dumont once operated a ferry; and yet another ten miles to where a coulee follows a northwesterly direction towards the river. At the bottom of the fifty-foot deep coulee, or ravine, runs a creek. Or rather, it runs in spring from the melting snows; for the rest of the summer it is but a series of pools, with the odd beaver track to be seen in the muddy stretches.

This is Fish Creek, where on April 24, 1885 Gabriel Dumont and a handful of rebel warriors demonstrated their skill in guerrilla warfare against a militia of about seven times their number. It was with regard to this second ravine that Dumont had declared he would treat the enemy like buffaloes herded to the pit.

Major-General Sir Frederick D. Middleton, 1885.

It had been almost a year since a Metis delegation had persuaded Riel to return from Montana in order to express Indian and Metis grievances over land claims and a fast-disappearing way of life. The Dominion Government had been lethargic and/or indifferent in reacting to Riel's petition. The result

Dumont had declared he would treat the enemy like buffaloes herded to the pit.

was that by the spring of '85 some violent confrontations had already taken place: Dumont had forced the North-West Mounted Police and Prince Albert Volunteers to retreat at Duck Lake on March 26; four days later Indians had laid siege to Battleford farther west; and the day after that some members of Big Bear's band had massacred nine people at Frog Lake.

The Dominion Government, upon hearing of the Duck Lake disaster, dispensed troops to Qu'Appelle and had Major-General Frederick Middleton organize an army of militiamen there to put down the Rebellion. April for them was one of the cruellest months to begin a campaign. The river was filled with floating ice after spring break-up, making the waterway almost useless as a transportation route. Land transport, on the other hand, had to be through snowy slush and mud with not enough new prairie grass burgeoning up to feed the horses.

Middleton not only had to see to the training of several hundred men, most of them raw recruits from the cities of Eastern Canada, but also to hiring teamsters (at $10 a day) to move supplies. On April 6, Middleton led his troops out of Qu'Appelle towards Batoche, some 200 miles to the northwest. He hoped, by striking at the rebel headquarters there, to put a quick end to the uprising.

It was 10° below zero (Fahrenheit) that day, and next morning the thermometer dropped to 23° below. The men, stumbling out of their tents in the frosty dawn, had to chop the tent pegs out of frozen ground, before breaking camp and moving on.

Middleton decided to divide his forces, leaving a column on each side of the river.

Movement was slow. The first day had seen a progress of only eleven miles, and for the next ten days the men found themselves both scraping over terrain like iron because of the frost—and sinking knee-deep in ice-cold water. Firewood was difficult to scrounge on the plains, so that not only hay had to be carried in their wagons.

At the end of this travail, the troop had passed through the Touchwood Hills, continued on to Humboldt, and then struck out west, arriving at Clarke's Crossing. This was the site where the Dominion telegraph line, which was constructed in the previous decade en route from Selkirk on the Red River to Edmonton, crossed the South Saskatchewan River.

Middleton was now about 40 miles short of his goal. By now he commanded a force of 800 men,

Trail winding through Fish Creek ravine, where the battle took place.

several groups of reinforcements having lately caught up with him. However, he did not have the support of Lieutenant-Colonel William Otter's force of 500 strong which was supposed to have met him here, arriving by steamboat from Swift Current. The siege of Battleford made it necessary that Otter go to that community's relief.

Besides the raw recruits, many of whom had never fired a gun, Middleton did have some experienced men on his staff. Major Charles Boulton, who had originally been sentenced to death by Louis Riel before being spared during Riel's first Rebellion at Red River (1870), was heading a troop of scouts. Captain John French, brother of the first commissioner of the N.W.M.P., had a similar assignment. Lord Melgund, who had previously served in Afghanistan and Egypt, was present. He would later be Governor-General of Canada, as the Earl of Minto. Also at hand was Lieutenant-Colonel C.E. Montizambert of the permanent artillery and Captain James Peters, who commanded a force of gunners. The total army had four cannon at its disposal.

It was at Clarke's Crossing that Middleton decided to divide his forces, leaving a column on each side of the river. He reasoned that should Riel's forces scatter, he could more easily pursue them. Furthermore, if the river must be crossed, it was easier and safer to do so now rather than during the duress of battle. Four days were needed to accomplish this task, for even with the Crossing's

scow and another one available, the men had to contend with slippery banks and blocks of ice on shore.

On April 23 Middleton continued his march towards Batoche. Accompanying his own division on the right bank were Boulton's Scouts; while ferried across to the other side, and now marching in a parallel column, was the division including Melgund and also Montizambert, the officer in command of it. In between the two columns floated a tethered scow, to be used for further transportation if necessary.

Back at Batoche, Riel and Dumont knew precisely what Middleton was doing. Indeed, one of the militia's teamsters was a rebel spy. Dumont would have liked to harass the army while it was still encamped at Clarke's Crossing, but Riel refused. However, knowing of Middleton's plan to march north from the Crossing, Dumont then convinced his leader that the time was ripe for the kind of fighting they could do best—raid and ambush. It was now or never.

Riel's forces had at one time that spring totalled some 450 strong, although only two-thirds of that number were armed. In the interval of waiting since the Duck Lake affair, some of the men had grown restless and drifted away; others, hearing of the militia's advance, also left. The rebel forces now were decimated by more than 100, but still, sufficient numbers remained to execute Dumont's plan.

Accordingly, later on the day of April 23, Riel and

Dumont with 100 armed warriors rode out to Fish Creek. Some 40 men stayed behind to guard the headquarters, should troops from Prince Albert mount a surprise attack. Perhaps those staying behind became fidgety; at least, after a short time, they did send couriers to catch up with the band of warriors in order to tell them that police scouts had been seen and an attack was feared.

The Dominion Government had been lethargic and/or indifferent to Riel's petition.

What to do? Riel was all for going back, and so were many men. But Dumont was adamant. Riel had thwarted him before from taking full advantage of his military position at the Battle of Duck Lake. Now Dumont was determined to press on. The result was that Riel returned with 50 men for the defence of Batoche. (The threat of immediate attack there, by the way, proved to be a false alarm.)

At Fish Creek, Dumont stationed his men. The site suited his purposes perfectly. To the south of the coulee was a flat plateau, a clearing, from which Middleton would approach in full view. The trail from Clarke's Crossing to Batoche then led through the ravine, which was wooded. Dumont placed some men below the northern lip, some near the bottom along both sides of the trail. The men, already screened by poplar trees and willows, threw up a log or two in front of them which would facilitate their sharp-shooting purposes. Chiefly ensconced west of the trail was a party of Teton Sioux while Dumont's fellow Metis lay in hiding to the east.

The rebel force was indeed a varied mixture of warriors—and not only in race: old men engaging in prayer, a continuation of that devotion led by Riel during a rest stop on the journey down (one individual reportedly clutched his crucifix during the whole of the succeeding engagement); young men, hardly more than boys, feeling within their being the thrill of a great adventure and then finding that emotion alternating with downright fear; Sioux Indians in war paint, stimulating more fear in others, it would seem, than knowing it themselves. The arms of these men were as varied as their own appearance. Muzzleloaders, shotguns, and, in some cases, horseshoe nails for bullets were part of their equipment.

"The Battle of Fish Creek" by J. de H. Haig.

Dumont, himself a fearless burly individual and an excellent horseman, did not stay in the ravine but, with 20 other marksmen, rode out early on the morning of April 24 in order to reconnoitre Middleton's camp, just a mile to the south. Already by 6:30 A.M. the militia column on that side of the river was moving ahead, while Montizambert's division on the west bank waited for Melgund to ferry a load of hay across from the other side on the awkward-handling scow.

Middleton's division of the split-up militia had some 400 men. They now approached the fateful ravine with Boulton's Scouts ahead of the main contingent. Dumont and his crackshots held up in a

They had spotted the fresh hoofprints left there by some of the rebel party.

bluff to the west of the trail when they heard the screeching of wagon wheels and the muffled thunder of horses' hoofs up the road. Dumont's little crew was hoping to harry or lead the enemy, like so many buffaloes, into the "pit" where rebel guns were waiting.

Then Dumont saw the militia scouts pull up short and look down at the road. He had spotted the fresh hoofprints left there by some of the rebel party—not by Dumont and his selected marksmen to be sure, for they had been careful to avoid the sandy trail, but by some of the others who in high spirits had been racing their ponies along this course in their leader's absence earlier that morning.

Boulton's Scouts were somewhat wary. Was there a large rebel force nearby? Dumont and his men in the bluff lost no time now. A fusillade of shots poured out from the trees, and the soldiers, turning in that direction, saw puffs of smoke rising above the stand of poplars.

Immediately they swung off the trail toward their assailants and returned the fire. The battle had begun.

Since the Scouts showed no signs of retreating to the main force, Dumont now tried to lure them into his trap. The Metis quickly mounted and galloped down into the coulee. But the Scouts, now dismounted and, flat on their stomachs, stayed on the plateau, exchanging shots with their hidden enemy, waiting for their column to catch up. Several of their men were hit. For their own part, they had gunned down an Indian in full war paint who chose that time to expose himself in a defiant war dance.

Dumont had lost the element of surprise he had counted on, but he still had the superior field position. The only trouble was that at the first sounds of gunfire, many of his force had fled—more would desert later that morning—so that finally he had but some 50-60 warriors left. One consolation was that the fleeing men would bring the news of the onslaught to Batoche, and hasten the gathering of reinforcements.

The militia now spread out on both sides of the trail, not too far back from the lip of the ravine. When the soldiers advanced to the edge, they were picked off by the sharpshooters below. They could

do nothing but fall back, then try another advance. Each advance meant more casualties for them, with little damage done to the enemy.

The green troops were getting their first taste of blood, and it was not a pleasant thing: comrades dying on the field, their wounds often more than neat bullet holes, being instead jagged and torn by the rebels' crude homemade ammunition. Hospital tents received a steady stream of victims borne in on stretchers or else dragged there from the front line.

At the ravine the sniping continued. Middleton had two cannons directed at the rebel force, but since those men had the near slope as protection, the shells lobbed at them had little effect. Indeed, the soldiers in loading the artillery made excellent targets. On the other hand, the best targets that the militia had were halfbreed and Indian ponies which could not very well be concealed as their owners were. Fifty-five of the animals were shot.

Middleton could do little but move among his men, trying to instill courage among his flustered recruits by his own coolness. For his pains, a bullet whistled a hole through his fur cap. Meanwhile Captain Peters continued at intervals to set up camera equipment which he had brought along. Never before this day had battlefield photographs been taken in Canada, and once the conflict settled down to a steady pattern after the excitement of the initial skirmish, he took several invaluable pictures.

Back in the ravine, those rebels that had stayed to fight were in good spirits. Dumont's brother struck up a French War chanson, once sung by Napoleon's army in derision of the enemy they were battling

Middleton's forces eventually leaving Fish Creek for Batoche.

under the British Duke of Marlborough. The Metis, as they took up the song for each chorus, gained fresh courage. When Captain Peters led some soldiers into the ravine to dislodge the rebels from hiding, it was the uniformed militia who had to retire, with the loss of three killed and five wounded.

Gabriel Dumont felt some diversionary tactics were called for. Middleton had enough men to outflank the rebel band and possibly to surround the Metis and Indians in their own trap. The clouded sky boded a heavy rain, so that if Dumont's new plan was to prove effective, it should be carried out now.

Memorial cairn at Fish Creek today. Sixteen men lost their lives here on April 24, 1885.

With a few Metis he skirted under cover up the creek bed, crawled up the bank, and set fire to the prairie, upwind from the militia. The dampened grass and brush sent up huge billows of smoke drifting down upon Middleton's lines. Dumont's fighters took advantage of this screen, coming out of their former hiding places to harass the enemy at closer range.

The army line held, however, and its leader here made use of his teamsters, telling them to put out the advancing fire. And as the smoke cleared, the rebels who had taken part in the skirmish faded back into the ravine.

Thus the day wore on. The sky became more heavily overcast, and a mist of rain gave way to a steady drizzle. Middleton by this time had more men at his disposal. The second column on the other side of the river had been aware of what was happening from the very beginning, for it had heard the opening shots, but the unwieldly scow proved as cumbersome in ferrying troops here as it had been earlier at Clarke's Crossing. Again there were the obstacles of muddy slopes, ice, and the river current to contend with. Nonetheless, the scow, capable of carrying only 60 men according to Middleton's report, ferried across several times so that finally 250 men, the other two cannons, and some wagons and horses came across.

The newcomers wanted to charge the ravine, but Middleton ordered otherwise. His casualties had been heavy, and he didn't wish to risk further bloodshed.

Towards evening Dumont, too, received reinforcements. His brother Edouard rode up from Batoche with a force of 80 men, but by then the battle was for all intents over. Middleton ordered his troops to withdraw to a safer site nearer the river, where through the night the surgeons looked after the wounded. Forty-eight soldiers had been wounded that day, and four of those died, now totaling ten as the number dead, six having been killed in battle.

To further the total misery, the rain had changed to snow, and while the tents of the army camp kept out the wet, they did not keep out the cold. Night was upon the cluster of dispirited soldiers. Wounded men were moaning; others were trying not to listen or else trying to hear instead any sounds which might suggest a possible surprise attack in the darkness. The guerrilla rebels might sweep down upon them at any time.

But Dumont, it seemed, had had enough action as well. His force had fared considerably better than had the government troops. It had suffered only six fatalities—four killed outright and two mortally wounded. These dead and wounded he now took back with him to Batoche. The dead were buried in the church cemetery there.

Middleton's dead were buried near the battle site, with a pile of stones and a cross of peeled poplar poles to mark the graves. The wounded were eventually transported by a long caravan of jolting wagons to Saskatoon, after much waiting for a steamboat to arrive and assist with the task. The steamer, the *Northcote,* did not appear until May 5. Middleton's army had remained all this time at their Fish Creek camp, frustrated and restless, and it was not till two days later still that they marched ahead to their original destination, Batoche, and eventually quelled the uprising.

Gabriel Dumont had not exactly treated Middleton's men like buffaloes, but his small band of warriors had so badly shaken the larger government force that the militia had been forestalled in their onward march by two whole weeks! ⊕

GOLDEN GHOSTS OF GRANITE CITY

by Doreen Janko

Granite City sits, and the cold snows of winter pile up around its doors and the hot sun of summer shimmers in heat waves that roll down the mountain-side to the cool and shady banks of Granite Creek, and the tumbling waters of the Tulameen River.

Granite City sits with only chipmunks disturbing the sleeping ghosts of greater days, when gold glittered in the gravel of the creek. Granite City sits in passive silence: little is left of the 1885 boom-town: rotting timbers, topless cabins, tilted privies, an aimless 'boot hill,' and bachelor buttons that bloom blue as a July sky.

Granite City sleeps a mile from the Coalmont bridge, a scant ten miles west of Princeton, British Columbia. A cowboy, Johnny Chance, found gold in

Granite Creek in July 1885, and for a brief, brilliant moment Granite City became B.C.'s third largest city, following Victoria and New Westminster in size, but, according to all reports, far surpassed them in

...rotting timbers, topless cabins... bachelor buttons...bloom as blue as a July sky.

wild exuberance and lawlessness. It's told that 'everyone carried a revolver in his belt;' more probably, only a few cowboys and ranchers were armed. However, the gun-toting prospectors on Granite Creek were wild enough to raise the eyebrows of the miners who heard the cry of 'Gold'

Granite City today.

and came rushing from the Cariboo and the Kootenays to the valley of the Tulameen. The cowboys, like Johnny Chance, spent much of their time galloping up the creeks and back, seeking and finding some surface gold. History leaves the impression that these men, while delighted to discover gold, really had little inclination to dig-in and work for the precious metal. Certainly on that warm July day in 1885, Cowboy Johnny Chance had only one interest: cooling his feet in a bubbling creek.

It was hot, too hot to look for a few grouse for the evening meal, even though, as cook for the crew, it was the least Johnny Chance could contribute to his camp. It was almost too hot to even bother picking up those bright yellow pebbles down there in the water, below his feet. But, what the hec' ... and Johnny lazily wiggled his big toe around one of them, and slowly brought it within arms reach. Even when he realized it was gold, and there was more, just a-lying there, in the creek, he didn't leap up and shout "Eureka!" or "Gold!" Instead, Cowboy Johnny Chance casually picked up several more gold nuggets, and slowly strolled back to camp to show his friends. It was a hot day...a very hot day on Granite Creek, and gold was where you found it.

By the end of September, two and a half miles of Granite Creek had been staked.

And find it, they did. By the end of September, two and a half miles of Granite Creek had been staked. There was even a report that Cowboy Johnny Chance was getting as much as seventy-five dollars a day from his claim; but then, by September the weather wasn't quite so warm, and a fella could get a little work done, in reasonable comfort!

At the height of its success, Granite City boasted thirteen hotels, with all the accompanying services offered by the boom-town host of the 1880's. There were grocery stores and blacksmith shops, a shoe-maker, a drug store, a couple of jewellers, and people: people living in tents, people building cabins, people like a Swede named Johanssen.

Swede Johanssen spent two years in Granite City mining for gold; two years of working a claim on the creek, sluicing pay-dirt by the shovel-full, and panning down each clean-up from the sluice-box to carefully recover every flake, every color, every nugget. Like everyone else on Granite Creek, Swede Johanssen was finding a silver-colored metal with his gold. Unlike everyone else, he was saving it, tossing the white gold, piece by piece, into an old bucket. Who knows why? Perhaps he thought it might come in handy sometime; maybe he was just frugal; almost certainly, he had no idea that the silvery metal was platinum, and worth a fortune in its own right.

Swede Johanssen called it quits one day, and packed up to move on. He cleared out his cabin, gave his few sticks of furniture to a neighbor, packed a few supplies, folded his bed-roll, and as he walked out the door for the last time, the bucket containing the white gold caught his eye. Before he left Granite City, the story goes, Swede Johanssen buried that bucket of platinum in a shallow spot, south of the cabin, visible from the doorway.

Swede Johanssen moved on to the Kootenays, they say. He never came back to Granite City. Perhaps a new gold field lured him to greater riches. Maybe the love of a lady settled this roving miner into a comfortable lifestyle that held him for the rest of his natural days. In any case, his storied bucket of three hundred ounces of white gold—platinum—is still buried at Granite City, south of his cabin, in a spot visible from his door. So which is the Johanssen cabin? Does it still stand? Or was it burned in the Granite City fire of 1907? You can come and dig. Others have dug before you. You'll find broken bottles, rusting tobacco tins, an old pair of shoes with a newspaper in the soles, a bottle cap, maybe, or even a miner's pick. You can use a metal detector, or just dig in a spot that hasn't been turned over, and you just might find that bucket of platinum at Granite City.

There are facts that say the buried treasure could be there; facts that you might find useful in justifying your search: platinum occurs in quantity in only two placer areas in the world, one is the Amur River in Russia, the other is the Tulameen River, just below Granite Creek. Mining records of the area mention that platinum was recovered in fair amounts from the placer gold claims on Granite Creek. There are people alive today who remember, as youngsters in the area, playing with little pots of white gold, very much as children at the seashore collect and play with shells. And, in the depression years of the 30's, many made a living burning old prospectors cabins in the Granite Creek area, and sifting the ashes for the platinum that had been thrown away. In any case, those are the facts, and the story of buried treasure, at Granite City.

Today, Granite City survives in spite of the 1907 fire. The few old buildings that remain are weathered and rotting, but still standing with a steadfastness that outlasted even the most dedicated of the gold-seekers. The individual miner gave way to the massive dredge that re-routed Granite Creek, sucked gold from its gravel, and left in its path piles of tailings.

...Johanssen buried that bucket of platinum in a shallow spot, visible from the doorway.

Granite City survives today, as the Gold Rush of the 70's sees new claims staked along the creek. The sleeping ghosts of greater days are hearing again, the sounds of shovels in the gravel, water in sluice-boxes, and the quiet swish of pay-dirt in a pan. The bachelor buttons still bloom, blue as the summer skies, but today, the July sun catches and reflects the metallic gleam of the new stakes with their precise descriptions inscribed by modern prospectors...many, no doubt, as dedicated as Swede Johanssen; and some, just perhaps, destined to be as lucky as Cowboy Johnny Chance. ⊕

Granite City today.

Granite City today.

JOY IN THE WILDERNESS

by Jay Myers

Wild animals of the forest growled with intimidation. Bears destroyed the wheat crops. Wolves killed the sheep. Foxes preyed upon the chickens and lambs. Within each household there was constant anxiety of the threats of wild animals and possible unfriendly Indians. And the only defense was the flint-locked army musket.

It was the autumn of 1796. A caravan of covered wagons forged a trail north from Pennsylvania, making its way across the frontier at Niagara to the head of Lake Ontario, then along the northern shore to "Muddy York," the site of present-day Toronto. In 1796, York was a tiny village of only a few inhabitants, situated on the margin of the wilderness.

Jacob Cummer and his wife Elizabeth were among the travellers from Pennsylvania. They followed a trail through the heavy pine forest, surveyed and cleared the previous year by Governor Simcoe for the construction of his road known today as Yonge Street. The Cummers travelled on a distance of four miles to a point now determined as Eglinton Avenue in Toronto. Here, Jacob Cummer built a log shelter, passed the winter months of 1796-97, then made his way some six miles further north reaching a point known as Cummer's Settlement. Today, it is known as Willowdale, Ontario.

Neighbours were few and far between. To have grain made into flour, one had to journey forty-five miles on horseback, an excursion that could take as long as a week to complete.

On a very cold sobering day in November, a day of a north wind the black of winter's finger, Jacob Cummer had journeyed on horseback for such a purpose, leaving his wife Elizabeth alone with a small child lying in a crude home-made crib. Just as the sun was drowning beneath the horizon, a visitor made his way to Cummer's lonely log cabin.

The visitor was an Indian of idle disposition, yet a model of symmetry and strength. He moved his barrel-chested frame into the sparsely furnished room and sat down at the table while Elizabeth Cummer looked on, pursing her lips together in fright. The stranger's arm hung limp as if he had just carried a heavy load a great distance, and his trousers bagged noticeably between his truncated legs. He stared at Elizabeth for some time. The look of hunger and the need for warmth oozed forth from his parched face. Yet, not a word was uttered between the two.

Elizabeth set the table for two and began preparing a meal. The Indian's sallow face stared relentlessly at her long bladed knife as if the need for it was imperious.

The redness in his cheeks soon disappeared and his features began to take on a more human look, showing a tinsel of sentiment.

Elizabeth took her place by the table and ate slowly, gripping the utensils with cold, shaking fingers, knowing full well that the Indian's lonely gaze was directed at both herself and the knife. Still, not a word passed between them.

The young woman's heart pounded, seeming as loud as hammer strokes, yet she was prepared and awaited what she thought to be the inevitable. If she was to die by the blade of her own knife, there was little she could do to avoid it, but she cared little for herself. Her life was centered around her son and husband. It was her child for whom she feared the most.

The Indian shuffled in his chair. Elizabeth's face grew pale and sickly. Her face tightened and her frame became rigid. The knife seemed to glitter from the energy radiating from the stranger's gaze. Utter silence. The Indian finished his meal. He reached across the table and took the knife. He looked up at Elizabeth and in one swift movement, left the log cabin without a word and disappeared through the grays of early evening.

When her husband returned, Elizabeth told him of the encounter, yet the Indian was not seen again until almost a year later.

Once again it was November. A light layer of powdery snow caressed the ground around the Cummer home. The figure of a man approached from the distance. His arms held something close to his chest. Elizabeth beckoned her husband and the two of them awaited the arrival of the stranger.

A knock came to the door. Then complete silence. Jacob Cummer walked to the door and waited. His wife remained in the far corner of the room. Jacob Cummer opened the door. In the silhouette of a brilliant sunset stood the Indian, holding in his cold, rough hands a cradle, carved out of wood with the very knife he had taken a year before. He had heard that the Cummer's infant son was the first white child born in the wilderness north of Muddy York, and came bearing the humble offering.

Elizabeth came forward, took the stranger's gift and the swift passage of a smile curved the lips of the Indian.

The knife was returned and the Indian left without ceremony.

Placing a fresh blanket in the crib, Elizabeth Cummer lowered her young son gently into the new bed.

Jacob and Elizabeth held each other tightly and cried quietly with joy!

THEY ALSO SERVED

by Rosa James

In the mid-1600's there was a small number of French immigrants in Quebec who had come over with the first French missionaries. Their children were running wild because the mothers were overworked with cooking, weaving, knitting and all the other labors connected with pioneer home-steading, and the little boys and girls unfortunately knew no more than their prayers.

To right the situation, the missionary priests begged the educated ladies of France for help and the first to hear and answer the call were three nuns, three hospital sisters and a wealthy young French woman. These were the first teachers, nurses, social workers and religious sisters to come to New France.

Young Canada was fortunate that the pioneer women of Quebec and later of Ville Marie were of such calibre. Their self-sacrifice and magnificent efforts have been almost entirely overlooked by historians. Today we reap the benefits of their self sacrifice and work, but how few of us realize it.

Many of the women who came to Canada from France were very religious, their vision fixed on the

The missionary priests begged the educated ladies of France for help.

way of the cross. They would do and die to attain their goal—the saving of the savage. These first women missionaries who came from civilized comfort to savage misery did so according to the dictates of their own conscience and to their understanding of Christian reasoning. They were sponsored by the high born wealthy French families and by the Queen of Austria.

A small merchant ship sailed across the Atlantic Ocean with three priests and eight women on board. The women were Mother de l' Incarnation, Madame de le Petrie, Mother St. Joseph and Mother Cecile, a wealthy young French woman and three hospital sisters, one of whom was Jeanne Mance.

They reached Quebec in August 1639 and fifteen days after they arrived a grand procession was held in Quebec. Indians in full dress led the procession, followed by the priests and the French population. There was a feast, and after this an Algonquin Chief spoke. He begged the French leaders to help them build houses, to teach them how to grow corn and vegetables and cultivate the land. He said, "We wish to believe in God. The words thou hearest are not mine. I am the mouth of all my brethren here. We want help."

Next, an Abenaki Indian spoke. He appealed for the same help, saying "Do not deceive us. I go to my home where the sun stands in the middle of the sky. When I come back the snow will be on the mountains. I will come to see if thou sayest the truth, if thou hast men to help us that we may no more live in the woods like beasts."

They wanted to know how to save their babies from dying.

Helen Champlain was the very first white woman pioneer. She fed, washed and taught a few Indian children. When they returned to their homes clean and fed, the Indian mothers wanted to know more, so the sisters decided to try to get the French and Indian women together. A time and place was arranged. The French women arrived first, then the Indian women with their faces made up with bear's grease and soot. They wanted to know how to save their babies from dying, how to keep them clean and feed them. So every week on a certain day these Indian women learned the rules of health and sanitation. Their children learned to read and write.

When the women went back to their camp after the meetings and told their men, they too wanted their children to have a better life so to encourage them to attend the meetings the sisters always had a cauldron of Sagamite ready and as many as eighty Indians, hideous in their warpaint, would squat around to be fed. The concoction was made up of a bushel of black plums, twenty-four pounds of bread, a gallon of Indian meal or ground peas, a dozen tallow candles and chunks of fat pork all well boiled together.

This meeting was called the Institute.

The men began to grow fields of maize, beans, squash and sunflowers. They stored the corn, beans and squash in communal log houses and in grain chests made of bark or in underground bark–lined pits. Cooking oil was made by boiling sunflower seeds in water and skimming off the oil.

The sisters' living accommodation was a shed

until the first Ursuline Convent and school was built. They had brought money from France to build a home, but it was spent feeding hungry Indian children.

More settlers came over from France and Madam de la Peltrie decided to go with her friend Jeanne Mance, the nurse, to Ville Marie. They arrived there in May 1642. Mother Marie de l'Incarnation was at Ville Marie, and kept a record of events. In 1644 she was ordered to return to Quebec, where she founded the first boy's college and girl's school. She was Canada's first school mistress and lived in the midst of religious and political bickerings.

Those first few years were full of terror, murder and invasion by enemy Indians. There were times when Iroquois invasions and terrorism were so frequent that the hair on their heads was threatened. The habitants did not dare venture far from home and farming was carried out under mounted guards. Savage war cries echoed and re-echoed throughout the land, and the tocsins warning struck fear among the bravest. Everyone was in danger, but Mother Marie and her workers were determined to win.

One day, a company of Hurons paid a visit to Quebec to see for themselves what the strange white men were doing and six or seven hundred braves in fifty canoes shot like arrows over boiling rapids and along rural rivers to see for themselves the great wigwams and the "captain of the day"—a clock whose fingers told the white man when to eat and sleep. They were also curious to see the cooking pots that could be set on a great fire and would not burn. After this they came every year. Mother St. Joseph learned the Huron tongue so that she could teach the Huron maidens who came to the convent school.

Farming was carried out under mounted guards.

Then came the massacre of the Hurons by the savage Iroquois and the 35,000 who escaped sought sanctuary within the shadows of the Ursuline Monastery. They gathered round the hearth fires and worried about the problem of food supplies.

Quebec at that time was the centre of military expedition and the fur trade. The steep trails which were the town's streets were marked by the footsteps of trappers, traders, soldiers and savages, rough men hardened by a life of training in the wilds where weaklings have no place and the women had to fight like men for their lives in surroundings of the crudest and most barbarous kind imaginable. Our Canada of today attests to their courage and determination.

Annie Edson Taylor and a replica of the barrel she used in her daring plunge.

DAREDEVIL IN A PETTICOAT

by Dwight Whalen

"Au revoir! I'll not say goodbye because I'm coming back." The spectators she addressed were not so sure, but Mrs. Annie Edson Taylor kept her word. She became the first person to plunge over Niagara Falls in a barrel and live to tell the tale.

Mrs. Taylor was a childless widow of 43 when she left her school teaching job in Bay City, Michigan.

Like other Niagara daredevils she had dreams of fame and fortune, and certainly would have found them in today's world of liberated women. But 1901 was a different world and October 24 would grant only fame—fortune, Mrs. Taylor learned, was not so easily won.

Her hair-raising journey began at 3 p.m. She was

"I'll not say goodbye, because I'm coming back!"

rowed, barrel in tow, from the American shore of the Niagara River to tiny Grass Island. Concealing herself in the foliage, she adjusted her clothing for a more comfortable ride. Her two boatmen discreetly placed themselves at the opposite end of the island, but they needn't have bothered. Modestly, Mrs. Taylor had removed only her hat and had raised her skirt to ankle length.

The boatmen guided her into her barrel, a one hundred and sixty pound vessel, four and one-half feet high and four feet wide in the middle. A one hundred pound anvil had been placed in the bottom to keep the barrel upright. There were straps inside to secure her, and cushions for padding, too.

When the lid was in place, the boatmen pumped air through a small opening in it using a bicycle pump. After an exhausting half-hour one of the men declared, "There! I've given her enough gas to last a week!"

To the astonishment of nearly all, the barrel was still intact.

The barrel was towed downriver to within one mile of the Horseshoe Falls, then the tow line was cut. In moments, the swift current of the Niagara River had captured the intrepid schoolmarm.

Thousands of spectators on both shores watched breathlessly as the sturdy barrel swept through the roaring rapids to the brink of the Horseshoe Falls. Awkwardly the anvil-weighted craft righted itself and plunged one hundred and seventy feet. The drop lasted three seconds but it seemed long seconds later before the barrel reappeared. To the astonishment of nearly all, it was still intact. But what of Mrs. Taylor?

Crewmen aboard the *Maid of the Mist* retrieved the bobbing barrel from the waters near the base of the falls. Her fate was learned when a crewman opened the lid. "Good God," he cried, "she's alive!"

Mrs. Taylor was delirious. "Did I go over the falls yet?" she asked repeatedly. She was battered and bruised and had an ugly gash behind her right ear, but in exchange for immortality she had driven a sharp bargain.

She was taken to her hotel room to rest with no thought of seeing a doctor, but not before she fired her timid press agent. The poor man fled to a bar when she had entered her barrel. He accepted it philosophically saying, "I'd expected to be out of work anyway."

That evening Mrs. Taylor gave the press an account of her adventure.

"I was tossed and pitched terribly in the rapids, but that was not so bad as the drop from the precipice. I struck on some rocks, I believe, and was hurled about and bumped frightfully. I could tell when the descent began by the feeling that something dropped out from under me. It's a terrible nightmare—I don't want to experience it again. I'd sooner be shot from a cannon."

With fame assured, Mrs. Taylor sought wealth on the lecture circuit, but her raspy voice and stern bearing made her an unappealing speaker. Soon, names like Marconi and the Wright Brothers were on everyone's lips, and Mrs. Annie Edson Taylor, "Queen of the Mist," as she had dubbed herself, was fast fading from memory.

Deciding to take her barrel on tour with her, she returned to Niagara to get it, but it had been moored at the *Maid of the Mist* dock so long it had rotted. In its place she used a duplicate barrel and stood beside it on a street corner in Niagara Falls, Ontario, endlessly recounting her tired story to passing tourists. Occasionally someone would purchase an autographed photo.

She fired her timid press agent who said "I'd expected to be out of work anyway."

She died penniless at the Niagara County infirmary in Lockport, New York, on April 29, 1921. Her last words, reportedly, were uttered in despair. "I did what no other woman in the world had nerve enough to do, only to die a pauper."

Annie Taylor lies buried in the Oakwood Cemetery at Niagara Falls, New York. her small tombstone bears this inscription:

Annie Edson Taylor
First To Go Over
The Horseshoe Falls
In A Barrel And Live
October 24, 1901

nnie Taylor is helped from her barrel by the crew of the
Maid of the Mist," after her plunge over Horseshoe
lls.

TEAMBOAT AND GRINDERS

The Teamboat "Sherbrooke"—1816.

Live horses provided the power that pulled the Teamboat "Sherbrooke" across Halifax Harbour—eight horses in single file, plodding round and round, in a round house, thirty-two hooves reaching in

"A floating merry-go-round."

mid-air until the massive bodies mastered the motion of the waves, and found their 'sea legs'.

Each horse was harnessed to an iron stanchion that extended from a large, horizontally arranged cogwheel. The wheel rotated a shaft which moved the single paddle.

"A floating merry-go-round", said Mr. W. H. Raddall, the most graphic writer of Nova Scotia history.

Sometimes a ninth horse was aboard, in case one became seasick, or dizzy, or both.

The teamboat made its first trip on Nov. 8, 1816, from Dartmouth to Fairbanks Wharf, Halifax, and continued in service until 1830, making four trips daily, and in winter, sometimes none.

In 1812, Halifax Harbour was the busiest port in

66

by Elsie Churchill Tolson

North America, but despite postwar prosperity, the Halifax Steamboat Co., founded in 1815, decided engines were too costly, so substituted team for steam.

Two ship's half hulls were joined. Both ends provided loading bows, so no turning was required. Stove heated cabins on both sides of the roundhouse balanced the comical outline, protected passengers from rain, and separated males from females.

The ferries between Dartmouth and Halifax have operated democratically—there have not been first or second classes, but, for 155 years there have been two sections, marked, Men, and Women. What is there about salt water? Now, they are designated, Smoking, and Non-Smoking!

A conch shell was blown to signal departure from Dartmouth. For four pence a passenger could sit in

Passengers in the bow were obliged to poke an iron pole through the skim ice.

the proper cabin, or throw a line over the rail and fish. Some anglers even filleted the fish and packed them in salt, while the more delicate passengers wrote letters to the paper complaining about the mess and slippery decks.

On days when the deep harbour water was choppy, the poor horses slid and lunged frantically, gripping for traction, while the boat drifted perilously. It was then the Skipper raised the big sail, and often, the topsail.

Sturdy, tubby boats supplemented the Teamboat. These were propelled by sidewheels, moved manually by cranks—they were called Grinders. But the racket they made was scarcely noticed in the teeming harbour filled with vessels, men-of-war, and paddle wheelers.

Ferries had been crossing since Feb. 3, 1752, when Governor Cornwallis granted a charter to John Connor, who agreed to operate two good and sufficient boats from sunrise to sunset, but never on Sundays, except one trip to accommodate churchgoers. (He was the man to whom Surveyor Morris referred, when reporting to Cornwallis that "John Connor, a one-legged (and possibly one-eyed) man, on February 6, 1753, returned with James Grace in a canoe with 6 Indian scalps.")

The first ferries were nothing but row-boats, and although Halifax Harbour never freezes, ice sometimes forms in Dartmouth Cove where the boat landed, so passengers in the bow were obliged to poke an iron pole through the skim ice, while the ferryman rowed.

The Teamboat was supplanted by steamers, and the first one made its rollicking way up the Basin, in

1830, to Bedford. Bedford Basin is a seven by four mile inner harbour that is approached from Halifax Harbour through the Narrows. It is a magnificent body of water, deep enough and large enough to have sheltered all ships gathering for convoy escort during wars.

On Jan. 21st, 1830, the first steamer ferry made its run. Never before had anyone seen a floating funnel belching smoke in Bedford Basin. Vantage points were black with people. A fine winter day further cheered the jovial excursionists, and the long expanse of ice free water encouraged Capt. Hunter to dash stylishly up the miles to Bedford.

Passengers enjoyed the two-and-a-half hour jaunt for 15 pence each.

On his return he made a sweeping arc past Millview, Birch Cove and Rockingham, ending with a triumphant circle around George's Island, sometimes tearing along at eight to ten miles an hour.

Passengers disembarked at Halifax Slip, having enjoyed the two and a half hour jaunt for 15 pence each.

The "Sir Charles Ogle", first steamer built and used in Nova Scotia, was a one-lane paddle-wheeler, fitted out with the first steam engine of its kind in Nova Scotia, rated at 30 H. P. In length the vessel was 108 feet, in beam width 20 feet, deck width 35 feet, and of 176 tons. Like the former Teamboat, it had two cabins for male and female passengers.

The vessel was built at Alexander Lyle's shipyard (established in 1813) at Dartmouth Cove, the first of three ferries built for ferry service. According to records, it had a life span of 65 years, very good for a steamer that used Atlantic Ocean salt water to make steam, with the result that tubes became clogged, and there were some lay-ups. These caused a wit of 1835 to advise people to don the diving apparatus that had been invented by Mr. Fraser of Halifax, and walk under water during the "naps" taken by the "Ogle".

Two days before launching, the boat had been nameless. Officials of the Steam Boat Company, hastily sent a note to Rear Admiral Sir Charles Ogle: "As the first steam vessel in Nova Scotia has been built during the period of your command upon the North American station, the Company avail themselves of this opportunity of expressing an opinion of the zealous, unremitting and effectual advantage which you have ever afforded to the navigation and commerce of this part of His Majesty's dominions. As a memorial of such an opinion they request permission to call their vessel the Sir Charles Ogle, a name which will long be respected in this Province." Signed, H. H. Cogswell, Thomas J. Jeffrey, Lawrence Hartshorne.

(One of the 25 shareholders was Samuel Cunard, and by 1840 he was President of the Company, and the famous Cunard Line was coming into eminence.)

Launching was at high tide, New Year's Day, 1830. The wedges were loosened, she slid down the greased skids, and jammed!

By night tide, Captains Boxer, and Travers, of His Majesty's Ships of War were there, with a large party of sailors, who launched her handily.

Passengers and teams were carried on Jan. 12th, and next day there was a whirl around George's Island, then the Ogle settled down to regular ferry service. There would be four trips an hour, as against four a day by the old teamboat. Fare would be 4 pence, and more for the occasional excursion.

The wintry day did not cool the enthusiasm of gentlemen sports, and for the first excursion on Jan. 21st, a large crowd had assembled. After waiting an hour, some went home, but regretted it later, for at 12 noon the Sir C. Ogle left with a flourish. Wind and tide were against her. The ebb at the Narrows was "at least 2 miles an hour," and a snow squall was giving 5 to 6 knots resistance, yet the excellent engine carried her through majestically.

Snow and slow speed gave the gentlemen an excuse to go below where they found the cabins commodious and "the gratification of the parties was not a little increased by the enjoyment of such refreshments as Mr. Keefler of the Exchange Coffee House had prepared."

Once the steamer had conquered the troubles in the Narrows, the sun came out, and the basin sparkled in all its glory.

Warmed and happy, and full of spirits of one kind or another, the passengers came out on deck to cheer lustily, and wave their beaver hats, as the steamer dashed to the Head of the Basin.

All served remarkable foods: "hot turkeys, smoking caribou steaks, reindeer tongues."

The first steamer excursion in 1830 initiated one of the most popular forms of recreation that was to continue on for 75 years. By 1830, there were three excellent, large and well patronized Inns in Bedford, Ten Mile House, Nine Mile Inn, and Mill House. All served remarkable food. For instance, this is one meal that was served at Nine Mile Inn, in 1827: "hot turkeys, smoking caribou steaks, reindeer tongues, pickled herrings from Digby, bear-hams from Annapolis, Noyeau, cherry brandy, Prince Edward Island whiskey."

After a sunny excursion along the beautiful shores of Bedford Basin, Bedford was the gold at the end of the rainbow, and then there was the moonlight voyage back to Halifax, with bands on deck playing dance music: all a part of early transportation in Nova Scotia.

The Steamer "Sir Charles Ogle"—1830

MICHILIMACKINAC
The Bloodless War

by William Silvester

In the northwestern-most corner of Lake Huron lies St. Joseph Island upon which, in 1765, the British built a small, nondescript fort. Passing virtually unnoticed to the outside world for many years, the fort became, in time, a way station for the North-West Company fur traders, and a small town sprang up around the palisade. But it was not until the War of 1812 was unleashed against Great Britain and her colonies by the United States that Fort St. Joseph came into prominence.

Forty miles to the south-west was a second fort, built on Mackinac Island by the British and ceded to the Americans following their Revolution. Known both as Fort Mackinac and Michilimackinac, depending upon the eloquence of the person speaking of it, it too remained in the back waters of North American history until the War of 1812.

Captain Charles Roberts was not a man to vacillate.

Paradoxically, though the Americans had been first to declare war in June of 1812, they seemed in no great haste to inform the commanders of the scattered garrisons of the fact. Therefore, it was the British at St. Joseph who first acquired the information and Captain Charles Roberts, 10th Royal Veterans Battalion, was not a man to vacillate when such an opportunity presented itself.

On 8 July, 1812, a messenger from Major-General Isaac Brock arrived at Fort St. Joseph with a letter dated 26 June, informing Roberts of the outbreak of hostilities and ordering an immediate attack on Michilimackinac; or, if this was not practical, then all effort must be made to secure St. Joseph in a defensive position. The following day a second letter arrived dated 27 June. Brock countermanded his first order. A third letter arrived on 10 July advising Roberts to proceed with the 'most prompt and effectual measures to possess himself of Michilimackinac', making use of local Indians and volunteer fur-traders of the North-West Company for the assault.

Hoping that the latest letter from Brock would be the last, Roberts began making preparations for the descent upon Mackinac Island. In typical bureaucratic style, a fourth letter arrived, dated 25 June, instructing Roberts to exercise 'the greatest vigilance and caution' and signed by the Adjutant General for Sir George Prevost, Governor-in-chief of British North America. Had it not been pointed out to Roberts that the letter from Brock post-dated Prevost's and thereby countermanded it in theory if not in fact, the operation might have come to a halt. Roberts, however, was eager to come to grips with the Yankee and decided to obey Brock.

The North-West Company immediately volunteered its services and as Prevost had insisted that Roberts 'afford every assistance and Protection Possible to Promote the Interests and Security of the North-West Company', he felt it his duty to accept.

The Nor'westers came forward with 180 employees. John Askin, Jr., a storekeeper at St. Joseph, raised 300 Chippewa and Ottawa Indians while Robert Dickson, another merchant and trader, brought in 140 Sioux, Winnebago and Menominee Indians. Though the actual number of Indians involved varies with different accounts, when added to the 45 members of the 10th Royal Veterans they comprised a formidable force. Michilimackinac, on the other hand, boasted less than 60 US regulars.

Still somewhat uneasy as to his course of action, due to the conflicting orders received, Roberts hastened as slowly as expedient to prepare the attack. On 15 July, his burden was lifted when a letter arrived from Major-General Brock, telling the Captain to use his own discretion.

Pausing to consider, Roberts must have realized that taking the defensive was out of the question. The stockade that was Fort St. Joseph was virtually indefensible and if he delayed and reinforcements arrived at Michilimackinac, the chances of British success in the west would be lost. The Indians wanted action and would drift away if it was not soon provided. Besides this, the Americans at Mackinac would soon get suspicious of the sudden burst of activity and the failure of some of the traders from Mackinac to return.

Shortly after having been informed of the declaration of war, Roberts arrested an American trapper on charges of spying when that man arrived at St. Joseph to trade but failed to produce anything to trade with.

Roberts was eager to come to grips with Yankee, and decided to obey Brock.

Roberts knew he could wait no longer and so on 16 July he embarked every man he could find into canoes and aboard the schooner 'Caledonia', graciously loaned by the North-West Company.

Perhaps one of the most important allies with Roberts was Robert Livingston, the local Indian agent for the British Government in Canada and manager of the North-West Company's trading depot at St. Joseph. Though not a regular soldier, he was more or less in command of the Nor'Wester contingent, spoke many Indian languages and was familiar with the country for hundreds of miles around. This included Fort Michilimackinac.

It was Livingston who recruited the Nor'Wester volunteers and scoured the Indian encampments for recruits. As the volunteers began drifting into St. Joseph, Livingston organized the undisciplined rabble into something resembling an army, though remotely, and served as liason between Roberts and his heavy-drinking, roisterous trappers. Roberts made no attempt to dissuade the independent traders and Indians from their carousing, insisting only on the most basic discipline.

An Indian from the Dakota recruits stole out of camp and headed for Mackinac to warn the Americans.

As Roberts and his army left St. Joseph some disquieting news was relayed to him by Livingston. Apparently, on the previous day, an Indian from the Dakota recruits had stolen out of camp and headed for Mackinac to warn the Americans of the ensuing attack.

The Indian, whose name has not been preserved for Posterity, reached Mackinac at about the same time as Roberts and his flotilla left St. Joesph. Lieutenant Porter Hanks, in command of the garrison at Michilimackinac, failed to realize the full import of what he was told and dismissed the Indian's tale as mere rumour. Just in case, however, he sent Michael Dousman, a farmer, fur-trader and American militia officer, to paddle to Fort St. Joseph and see what was going on.

Roberts, meanwhile, advanced in his flotilla, the canoes forming a protective shield around the 'Caledonia' as they sailed at a steady but leisurely pace along the Lake Huron shore. As night fell, the armada stopped at Goose Island to prepare supper, rest and await the dawn.

The canoe carrying Michael Dousman was sighted as the cook fires were being lit and the would-be spy was brought ashore. Dousman, indignant over his treatment, insisted that he was on his way to Sault Ste. Marie on legitimate business. Roberts, having heard that story on previous occasions from other wandering canoeists, informed Dousman that he was a prisoner of war and demanded his parole. Once Dousman consented, Roberts informed him of his plans and requested that he alert the inhabitants of the town about Michilimackinac and have them evacuate to ensure that no civilians were harmed in the battle to follow. Dousman agreed.

Hanks, meanwhile, still ignorant of the declaration of war, decided that the Indian who had warned him of the attack might be telling the truth after all and began preparations to repulse an Indian attack. It had not been made clear to him that regular British soldiers were included in the advancing army or that these soldiers were equipped with a 6-pounder field piece.

Shortly after supper, Roberts got underway again, fearing that any more delay might destroy the advantage of surprise which they still held. At midnight the flotilla arrived off Mackinac Island.

Dousman was put ashore to warn the village, accompanied by Livingston who was to assist in evacuating the town. This was accomplished with speed and a minimum of noise. The villagers were sent to the still-house at the far end of the island with the exception of a Doctor Day who took it upon himself to go instead to the fort and warn Hanks.

While the village was being evacuated, Roberts led his regulars, Indians and Nor'Westers to the north of the island which was protected by seemingly unscaleable cliffs. He ordered his men up and supervised the man-handling of the 6-pdr. By three o'clock the little army was in position on a hill overlooking Michilimackinac.

The Western Blockhouse, built by the British in 1780 at Fort Michilimackinac. by George Adrian.

It would have been obvious to the most casual observer that the fort was in no position to defend itself. The log stockade had been built on the smaller of two hills—a tactical error in itself—overlooking a harbour, which the fort's guns did not command. The interior of the fort consisted of several buildings, a powder magazine and three block-houses. A normal frontal assault would have proved bloody if not disastrous to the British for Michili-mackinac was a strong fortress made weak only by absurd geographical location.

The British 6-pdr. was trained on the magazine within the fort as Roberts awaited the rising of the sun. With the daylight, Dickson and Livingston left the hill and, accompanied by a party of Indians apiece, moved closer to the fort. At the same time, Roberts arranged for other Indians to wander about the hillside, stepping in and out of shadows to give the illusion that a massive array of natives swarmed over the hillside.

Roberts waited, letting the fears of an Indian massacre prey on the predictably frayed nerves of Lieutenant Hanks. Finally, at ten o'clock, Roberts sent one of his officers down to the fort to request Hanks' surrender. The officer was accompanied by the American fur traders who had been captured and held at St. Joseph's while the invasion was being prepared. Having been told by the British that the force from St. Joseph's had numbered over 1,000 regulars, Canadians and Indians, the traders naively gave this information to Lieutenant Hanks on the firm belief that it was indeed true.

Lieutenant Porter Hanks appraised the situation carefully. He knew that his garrison was badly undermanned and would not be able to withstand a lengthy seige. As he had just learned from the British officer that war had been declared, he saw no reason to expect early reinforcements. There was also the matter of the Indians. The massacre of prisoners was fast becoming a tradition amongst the tribes of the North-West. At the moment, Roberts had them under control, but once their fierce passions became aroused, no one would be answerable for what happened.

After due consideration, Hanks sent an officer to the hill to confer with Captain Roberts. Hanks requested that his men be accorded all the honours of war, that the property of private citizens be respected and that he be guaranteed safety from the Indians. Roberts agreed to all the proposals and Hanks surrendered.

At the time of the capitulation there were two British deserters in the garrison and they were immediately arrested as the British entered the fort.

All of the terms of capitulation were carefully honoured. Even the temptation of the two merchant vessels in the harbour was passed up and only military stores and some provisions were taken and these from the United States government's warehouse.

Once Lieutenant Hanks and his paroled officers and men were safely on their way to Fort Malden under protective guard, Roberts began to survey the latest addition to the British Empire. It did not take him long to decide that Michilimackinac was a fortress far superior to St. Joseph's. Knowing the importance of his achievement, Roberts determined to hold the American fort and sent only seven men back to Fort St. Joseph. These men would serve more as caretakers than defenders.

Michilimackinac was reinforced in September, shortly after the fall of Fort Detroit to General Brock, in another bloodless coup. The men came from Kingston, a sergeant and 25 rank and file, 10th Royal Veterans Battalion.

Though the Americans made an attempt to recapture Michilimackinac in July, 1814 they were unsuccessful and the first British conquest of the War of 1812 remained under the Union Jack until the Treaty of Ghent ended the war.

Geo. A. Guthbertson

RENEGADE ON THE RIVER

by Hugh F. Cochrane

The steamer had already docked at the isolated island, its great paddle-wheels silent. Stealthily the cut-throat gang crept through the darkness to within striking distance, then their bloodcurdling screams and yells filled the night air. They swooped on to the ship and its paralyzed and outnumbered crew with such suddenness that resistance was impossible. Within minutes they had seized control. Their leader struck a wide stance at the head of the gangway while the 70 passengers, some still in their night clothes, were herded roughly to the dock. In the dim light of lanterns his bulk loomed menacingly. His black coat billowed in the wind; his sharp features and deep-set eyes glared from under the wide brim of his black hat; even the six pistols and a bowie knife protruding from his belt seemed more threatening than the prodding swords and muskets that hurried the passengers on their way.

For fifteen years, "Admiral Bill" Johnston had complete run of the Thousand Islands region.

Such was the grim sight that greeted the passengers of the steamer "*Sir Robert Peel*" on May 29, 1839, at Wells Island in the St. Lawrence River, when they found themselves at the mercy of "Admiral Bill" Johnston, a renegade Canadian Patriot, pirate, and smuggler who for 15 years had complete run of the Thousand Islands region. While authorities on both sides of the river made half-hearted efforts to curb him, he turned the area into his own private preserve. His knowledge of the hidden coves, bays, and channels surpassed that of any other man.

William Johnston was born in 1782 at Three Rivers, Quebec. Later his family moved to what is now Ontario and settled near the town of Bath. It was here that Johnston got his first taste of the river. Starting out as a farmer, then as a merchant, he soon realized that the river had more claim on him

than any profession. While working in a nearby shipyard he finally succumbed to the lure of the river that was to dominate his very life.

In the beginning of the 1800's, Johnston was introduced to the lucrative trade of smuggling. From then on, even after forfeiting half of his property to the crown on his first conviction, he was never far from his beloved river and his chosen trade.

Johnston had an arrogance that most men either lacked or kept curbed. When he was called to serve in the militia against the Americans during the War of 1812, these same characteristics put him on a collision course with his superior officers. In short order he was brought up on a charge of insubordination and given a jail term to help him mend his ways.

But this was a man to be reckoned with. His powerful frame and equally powerful disposition were more than a match for his unsuspecting guards as they tried to carry out the court's sentence. Within a few days he had escaped their custody and was well on his way to the United States. There his arrogant attitude towards British authority won him quick friendship. To Americans, he represented proof that Canadians were only waiting for the day when they could be rid of British rule and join in a union with their cousins south of the border.

Yet neither politics nor nationalities mattered to Johnston. In his mind the border with its high tariffs on imported goods represented an opportunity for high profit to any who could deliver contraband to the north—and Johnston had every intention of picking up his share of it.

From a base at French Creek (now Clayton, N. Y.) he began smuggling tea, sugar, tobacco—anything on which the British government had sought to collect high taxes from Canadian settlers. When the American military suggested that he gather information on British troop movements he added spying and mail robbery to his activities and his business expanded.

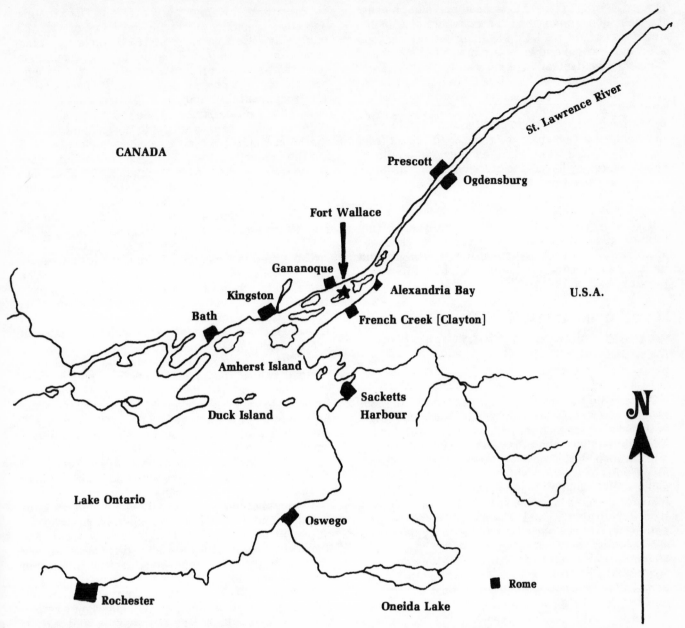

Sketch Map of "Admiral Bill's" pirating area.

Busy as he was, Johnston found time to father four sons, and a daughter who inherited her father's arrogance and determination. Her beauty and daring became known far and wide and she acquired the name "Queen of the Thousand Islands." His sons, too, had some of his character-

Neither politics nor nationalities mattered to Johnston.

istics. When they were old enough they joined him in the smuggling, yet none reached the "pinnacle" captured by their father.

Although he was a good father and first to aid his men whenever possible, "Admiral Bill", as he later became known, was ever vigilant about his own safety. He never trusted in the plans of others and he instructed those around him to be self-reliant. However, instruction is one thing, practice another. When Johnston and his crew were blown up on the Canadian shore during a heavy gale he left them on look-out while he went to scout the area. Before he returned, militiamen pounced on his crew and took them into custody. When he found himself without ship or crew, Johnston set out doggedly for home. Along the way he came on a battered canoe and for 36 hours paddled it across open water until he reached Sackett's Harbor on the American side of Lake Ontario. A short time later he was back at French Creek, and busily engaged in his activities among the maze of granite islands. Try as they might, the British revenue men were at a loss to keep up with his tricky maneuvers. Each time they thought they had him trapped, he slipped from their grasp and vanished into the uncharted channels and waterways. He always was able to keep one step ahead of the law and he always allowed himself just enough leeway to slip over into American waters.

When the Canadian Rebellion of 1837 began, Johnston was 55 years old, and though he was

75

himself a refugee from the same oppression, he saw the rebellion as a means for reviving some of his activities of 1812-1814. Gun-running had been a good source of income and to assure himself of a piece of the action he decided to pay a visit to William Lyon Mackenzie, leader of the Upper Canada Rebellion, who had escaped from Canada after the aborted uprising at York (now Toronto). Mackenzie was operating between Buffalo, N. Y. and Navy Island in the Niagara River which the rebels had seized from the British. The "Patriots", as they called themselves, were ony too glad to have Johnston join them. They even raised him to the rank of Admiral of the Eastern Fleet—a title which meant little since the fleet would consist mostly of whatever boats Johnston already had or could confiscate from Canadian sources. But the title also brought something he hadn't bargained for: it brought him under the command of others, something for which Johnston had no liking.

He allowed himself just enough leeway to slip over into American waters.

During the latter part of 1837 and on into 1838, groups of Canadian refugees and American sympathizers began to form around the Great Lakes. They called themselves the "Patriot Hunter lodges" and through these, money to finance the Rebellion, along with supplies, were funneled to further the cause of Rebellion in Canada. This fitted nicely with Johnston's plans and he gathered around him a band of brigands and freebooters who sought nothing more than adventure and an easy living. He soon replaced his old 6 oared boat with a sleek, light 40 footer with 12 long oars. Its outside was as black as the deeds he had planned for it, while into its red and yellow interior he loaded the most select and daring of his cut-throat crew. He was now prepared to venture into the most treacherous waters and move up to a higher quality of booty.

To his crew he was "Admiral Bill", and he ranged from 50 to 100 miles along the great St. Lawrence, his watery domain covering close to 300 square miles. He established secret hide-outs on Abel's Island opposite Alexandria Bay, close to Mallorytown on the Canadian shore, and another on Grindstone Island, a stone's throw inside the American Border. But his strongest point was established on a Canadian island that was hardly more than a granite outcrop in the middle of the river. This he fortified in such a way that any attempt to dislodge him would have to be launched through fast moving water while under fire from the island. He called it "Fort Wallace"—a name it has retained to this day—and he boasted that any 12 of his men could easily hold off a force of 200 attackers. He further went on to warn his enemies that he intended to"—sell his life for the dearest rate."

However, at this point, Johnston's plans suffered a setback. The Patriot Government of the Republic of Canada was bent on making strides. They needed victories to make their presence felt. Toward this end, they decided to get the invasion of Canada underway. By November of 1838, Johnston found himself in the position of having to take commands from the Generals of the Patriot Army, and he was ordered to take charge of a schooner loaded with 170 troops and their supplies. The original plan had called for a direct strike on the Canadian shore at Prescott, while flank landings to the left and right of the town would proceed in a pincers movement to cut the town off and establish a secure beach-head. In charge of the entire landing operation, but without the authorization of the Patriot leaders, was General John W. Birge. But he soon relinquished command to Colonel Niles von Schultz—excusing himself from the whole expedition on the grounds of "sickness".

The situation was one that Johnston didn't relish. And, whether it was by plan or accident, he managed to ground the schooner under his charge on a sand bar near the American shore. In an effort to free the vessel, the troops and supplies were transferred to another ship and the invasion proceeded without Johnston's help.

Unknown to the Patriot leaders, their plans were doomed before they had begun. The entire north shore had already been alerted and the small British steamer "Experiment" had been converted for use by the Royal Navy. When the "Experiment" stumbled on Johnston's grounded ship it immediately began a bombardment and the Patriot vessels "United States" and "Paul Pry" were forced to abandon the stranded schooner and make a hasty retreat.

Meanwhile, Von Schultz had reached the docks at Prescott unopposed but the generals got into an argument among themselves as to how the battle should be fought with the reduced forces available to them. Before they reached a decision their ship had slipped her lines and they were drifting downstream. Thus, by fate rather than choice, the rebel invasion took place at Windmill Point rather than Prescott which was now a mile and a half upstream.

What followed next turned out to be a week-long fiasco which ended with the entire invasion force having to surrender. Out of the 270 men in the force, 11 Patriot leaders, including Von Schultz, ended their lives on the gallows. Through it all Johnston had made no attempt to offer assistance or encouragement to the embattled Patriot forces. Instead, he was already directing his interest to other plans which would allow him to return to his buccaneering activities.

In the months that followed the disastrous Prescott raid, Johnston set about building a state of siege around the small Canadian communities along the St. Lawrence. They expected that at any moment another would begin. But where? Rumors became rampant. For a time it was thought that Kingston's Fort would be the target and it was said that Patriot spies had infiltrated the fort and were under orders to spike the guns just before the attack was scheduled to take place. When news finally came that Johnston's gang had left their base on Grindstone Island and were on the move, an alert was again spread along the north shore.

But their fears were groundless. The move from Grindstone Island had taken the rebel forces only as far as Hickory Island in the Navy Island Group. This they were able to "liberate" from the sole occupant, a widow, and, although they were within a quarter of a mile of the Canadian mainland, they were over 4 miles east of Gananoque and 25 miles east of Kingston.

Again, the operation was put under the command of another and Johnston found himself subservient to the orders of General Van Rensselaer. For most of his time on the island, Van Rensselaer remained in a drunken stupor while the Patriot troops became disenchanted and began to desert in wholesale numbers. When the General recovered enough to give the order to launch the invasion only 35 men of the original 300 remained. The attack was called off but when it came to removing the equipment and supplies, including three artillery pieces, for the trip back to Grindstone, hardly enough men could be mustered for the task.

The Battle of the Windmill had broken the spirit of the Patriots. Now, U.S. authorities were viewing the violations of the border in a different light. U.S. Federal troops were moved up to the border to put an end to these violations and when Van Rensselaer set foot on American soil he was arrested and brought to trial. For his part in the activities, he received a sentence of a year in jail and a $250 fine. After serving his time, he dropped out of all Patriot activities and never again took up the cause.

Johnston was glad to be rid of him. Now he could return to more profitable enterprises—ones that would put the clink of gold dollars, sovereigns, and doubloons back into the pockets of himself and his freebooters. He had already worked out a plan and as his first choice selected a rich plum, the "Sir Robert Peel". His spies had been keeping an eye on this wood-burning side-wheeled steamer as it plied the St. Lawrence and Lake Ontario. Now, news reached him that she was on her way with 30 cabin passengers and 40 more in steerage. The time was right for a rich haul of loot and Johnston set his men out on the river to watch for her.

News of his plan had also reached the Patriot leaders and they immediately offered him troops and assistance. The "Peel" would be a welcome addition to their small fleet, one that would enable them to carry out an attack against Kingston. Johnston, on the other hand, had some different ideas. He was quite prepared to carry out the attack on the "Sir Robert Peel" but using men he himself had selected. When the time came to move against the steamer, the Patriot troops who had been sent to assist him became lost among the maze of islands, while Johnston contentedly went on to do the job as planned.

Even so, the success of the raid on the "Sir Robert Peel" wasn't entirely due to Johnston's planning. In part, it was brought about due to the complete lack of caution on the part of the ship's Master, Captain Armstrong. Armstrong was an able master, though somewhat given to bragging and daring. Two days previous to the raid he had pitted his steamer against another in a race across Lake Ontario. He

had won the contest, but only at the expense of pouring turpentine over the firewood used to fuel the ship. The process started a fire that almost got out of control and consumed the vessel.

Now, as Armstrong brought his ship into the dock at Wells Island to replenish his supplies of firewood, a Mr. Ripley, keeper of the refueling depot, hurried to the ship to warn the Captain of danger. Several times during the early evening he had seen a suspicious boatload of men passing near the dock. He believed they might be part of the Johnston gang and he urged the Captain to cast off and seek safety on the Canadian shore.

"If there was no more than a hundred or a hundred and fifty, then I won't fear them."

Armstrong was adamant. "If there was no more than a hundred or a hundred and fifty, then I won't fear them," he replied boastfully. Then he ordered his crew to begin the task of loading the fuel aboard the steamer. Before they had finished the hour-long task, Johnston's men were on them. The "Sir Robert Peel" fell easy victim to the cut-throats and brigands.

Various figures have been suggested for the amount of loot taken that night, but a conservative estimate puts it close to $100,000. Some $80,000 of this was in gold specie which was being brought to pay the British troops, and the rest came from the pockets and valuables of the passengers. In all, a record haul for a night's work.

How much of this wealth found its way into the Patriot treasury is a debatable question. What is sure, is that before the raiders left the ship, they ransacked the cabins and luggage of the passengers, then set the ship afire and let her drift downstream with the current. The voyage was a short one, for the blazing vessel ran aground on a rocky shoal. While still burning, she capsized, and her engine became dismounted and burst through the hull. A few hours later the ship was a stark sight of twisted iron and charred timbers, one paddle-wheel raised clear of the water.

Johnston's decision not to save the vessel for the Patriot Fleet may have been dictated by a strong desire to get out of the vicinity as quickly as possible before news of the seizure reached authorities on either side of the border. As it was, one of the "Peel's" passengers escaped the island before morning and spread the news. Orders went out from Kingston, confining all Canadian shipping to port while a search was made for the raiders. Meanwhile, a rescue vessel was sent to aid the marooned passengers.

Of all the border incidents during the years of the Canadian Rebellion, none aroused the indignation that the attack on the "Sir Robert Peel" brought from both sides of the border. Public feeling ran so high that a determined effort was made to rid the river of the pirate gang. The British government posted a reward of $1,000 for information leading to the conviction of Johnston and his freebooters. American newspapers took up the cause and branded President Van Buren's administration as corrupt for not enforcing the neutrality laws. Within days, both sides of the river became active with troops and militia. But the crafty pirate and his crew of 13 who had carried out the attack, had already vanished into the labyrinth of the Thousand Islands. Ten days after the attack on the *"Peel"* Johnston and his gang struck a small settlement on Amherst Island, 40 miles to the west, near his old home at Bath. Six days later, they were foraging among the Duck Islands in Lake Ontario. Another 3 days and they had traversed the St. Lawrence's maze and were 80 miles to the east and close to Brockville. They were like a ghost wind moving in the night.

The 57 year old pirate now had proved himself master of his river. He returned to his base at Fort Wallace Island, yet no effort was made to dislodge him. During this time, his daughter dared the forces on both sides of the river and made several visits to see the old buccaneer. In later years, her boldness laid the groundwork for several novels written about the area.

Six months later, Johnston performed as expected: he made his escape.

But Johnston's sovereignty was nearing its end. One morning, he inadvertently walked into a trap in the bush near the American shore. True to his arrogance, he defied his American captors and dictated his own terms of surrender before he gave up the 12 shot Cochran rifle in his hand and the two pistols in his belt. He was taken under heavy guard to Ogdensburg, and then to Auburn to await trial. While U.S. Marshals set out to collect the evidence that would send him to prison, the wily Johnston slipped free from custody during the night. Again, rewards were posted for his capture, but he managed to reach Rome, N.Y. on foot before he was caught.

Since none of Johnston's activities had been directed against American citizens, the court finally decided to try him for violation of the U.S. Neutrality Laws. This brought him a sentence of a year in prison and a fine of $250. His daughter promptly came forward and offered to serve half of the prison term, but she was refused. Even so, six months to the day later, Johnston performed as expected: he slipped from the prison guards and made his escape, leaving behind dumbfounded authorities, desperately trying to explain their inability to keep the old pirate in custody.

With the aid of friends and sympathizers, "Admiral Bill" went underground while authorities scoured his old haunts and hide-outs. The conniving old buccaneer outsmarted them. Months later he resurfaced at the capitol in Washington to plead his case before President Harrison. By now, public opinion had reversed itself and "Admiral Bill" was a hero once more. With a pardon in hand, he returned to his beloved river. And, as if to crown his career in irony, he was given the post of lighthouse keeper on Rock Island—the very rocks on which the *"Sir Robert Peel"* had met her doom!

In the quiet of the lighthouse, memories of bygone adventures and excitement returned to haunt the old pirate. He soon gave up the light and opened a tavern where he could keep company with his old mates. Those who knew him during this period said that "Admiral Bill" still did an occasional smuggling job for his friends north of the border, but the jobs were all minor: the smuggler of old was feeling his age.

On February 16, 1870, at the age of 88, and in a French Creek Hotel owned by his son, "Admiral Bill" Johnston's colorful life came to an end. During his years he had seen his river change from a pirate's paradise to a tourist's delight. Typical of his old buccaneer bravado were the three islands which he came to own during the last years of his life—he named them "Ball, Shot and Powder". ⊕

Bill Johnston, pirate and patriot, who vowed to be a thorn in the side of the British—and succeeded.

THE BRATTON KIDNAPPING

by Anthony Appleblatt

A Carolina Ku Klux, as illustrated in "A Fool's Errand" by Judge Albion Tourgee.

On December 24, 1865, at Palaski, Tennessee, six former confederate soldiers were looking for amusement. They were bored with the tedium of small town life after the wartime excitements, and decided to form a "Hilarious social club." They called their social club the Ku Klux Klan, a name derived from the Greek word "kyklos" meaning circle. After choosing this mysterious-sounding name for their social club, the first Klansmen adopted an organization and ritual just as mysterious. Their meeting place would be called the "Den", and their officers would have such titles as wizards, dragons, cyclops, hydras, titan, furies, and night-hawks.

The "hilarious social club" was to be a society with a blood-curdling pledge of secrecy. Their code would be chivalry, humanity, mercy and patriotism. To celebrate the founding of their social club, the first Klansmen borrowed the idea of Hallowe'en disguises. They dressed up in robes made from bedsheets, hid their faces behind white masks and rode through Palaski. The recently-freed, superstitious Negroes who saw the mounted Klansmen that night believed they were the spirits of Confederate soldiers risen from their graves. The frightened Negroes fled to their homes in panic-stricken terror; and so, the Ku Klux Klan as an instrument of terror was born.

Through the fall and winter of 1866-67, the Ku Klux Klan outgrew the confines of Palaski and surrounding Giles county. Dens sprang up throughout Tennessee and across the state borders in Alabama and the Carolinas. Klan membership grew very quickly. Many members were bitter, violent men who were to use the Klan as an instrument to fight Reconstructionism imposed by the North.

At the first large Klan convention held in Nashville, Tennessee, the members declared their objective and purpose to be "the maintenance of the supremacy of the white race in this republic." At the same meeting, the gallant Confederate cavalry general Nathan Bedford Forrest became the Klan's first Grand Wizard.

Negroes and those who sympathized with reconstructionism became the targets of the Klan. The warnings and threats of the Klan turned into violence. Their victims were whipped, tarred and feathered, mutilated, raped, lynched and burned. The Klan dispersed the Negro militiamen and saw to it that Negroes did not vote in elections.

By 1869, Klan membership in the South was estimated to be in the hundreds and thousands, and Klan atrocities were mounting. In January of that year, General Forrest ordered the disbandment of the Klan and the burning of its records. Not only did he believe that the Klan had been perverted from its original purpose, but he was also repelled by its violent tactics. But despite his order, Klan violence and activities continued.

In 1871, a Congressional committee launched the first extensive investigation into Klan activities. Thousands of cases of torture and killing were uncovered. Congress passed a bill outlawing Klan activities. President Grant enforced martial law in two southern states, and in some cases, the right of habeas corpus had to be suspended. Public revulsion over the atrocities committed by the Klan, coupled with its supression by Federal laws and troops, broke the back of the Klan by 1872.

Canada is well known as a country which gave sanctuary to runaway Negro slaves before and during the American Civil War. But not so well known is the fact that after the Civil War, Canada became a haven for Confederate refugees and wanted Ku Klux Klansmen. Among the more notorious Klan leaders who sought refuge in Canada were General H.P. Mabry, wanted for murder in Jefferson, Texas; General Dandridge McRae and Colonel Jacob Froelich, wanted for murder in White County, Arkansas; Major James Avery, wanted for murder in Yorkville, South Carolina and Dr. J. Rufus

Bratton of Yorkville, South Carolina.

The Canadian government regarded these people as political refugees and even published a book of instructions for Confederate refugees to use in Canada. Because of this Canadian policy, the United States government was not able to secure the extradition of wanted Klansmen, and therefore resorted to kidnapping them. One such kidnapping was the Bratton case of 1872 which almost developed into an international incident.

On March 6, 1871 at Yorkville, South Carolina, Jim Williams, a Negro militia captain who had often spoken out against the Ku Klux Klan was murdered. Fifty Klansmen led by Dr. J. Rufus Bratton burst into Williams' home, dragged him out and lynched him on a nearby tree. Bratton himself placed the rope around Williams' neck, and before the Klansmen rode off, they attached a note to the hanging body which said: "Capt. Jim Williams on his big muster."

Extra Federal troops were sent into South Carolina. At a military investigation at Yorkville, it became apparent that Jim Williams was murdered by members of a Klan den called the Rattlesnake Den whose leader was known to be Bratton.

Dr. Bratton fled north, and succeeded in eluding any pursuers. He arrived in London, Ontario on May 21, 1872, where a friend of his, a Confederate refugee named Gabrial Manigault, gave him shelter. Bratton changed his name to James Simpson. He told people that he was from Alabama, and settled down to practice medicine.

Bratton was the epitome of a southern gentleman: about forty-five years of age, tall and gaunt, with greying hair. His charming manner soon gained him many friends, as well as patients for his practice.

Two United States police officers were soon on Dr. Bratton's trail. Federal detective and United States deputy marshal Joseph G. Hester, a specialist in hunting down wanted Ku Klux Klan terrorists, and S. B. Cornell, a police officer from Columbia, South Carolina arrived in London close on Bratton's heels. In London, the American detectives enlisted the services of Isaac Bell Cornwall, the local deputy clerk of the peace. Cornwall had been keeping the Confederate refugees in London under surveillance, and he pointed out Dr. Bratton to the American detectives.

On the afternoon of June 4th, Dr. Bratton stepped out from his rooms on Wellington Street for a quiet walk. A hansom cab approached him. Just as the cab reached Dr. Bratton, detectives Hester and Cornell suddenly jumped out and grabbed him. One of the detectives held Bratton down while the other chloroformed him. His hands were handcuffed behind his back and he was thrown into the back of the cab. The cab raced to the Great Western railway station. From there, he was taken by train to Windsor, across the border to Detroit, and then to Buffalo.

The American press was ecstatic on hearing the news of the kidnapping. One Detroit newspaper was headlined: "Hunted Down—Capture of a Notorious South Carolina Ku Klux Klan Outlaw." The Detroit Post declared that Bratton is "one of the most desperate of the horde of outlaws and desperadoes whose acts of bloodshed and violence have filled the measure of repulsion for months past."

In Canada, there was a sense of outrage. The Canadian press demanded action from the government. The Toronto Globe stated that, "It is the duty of the Government to act promptly and decidedly in this matter, and demand that the stranger taken with violence from under the protection of the British Flag be returned unharmed and rendered secure from further molestation...Official outrages of the above nature must not be tolerated if we desire to maintain the national honour unsullied." The London Advertiser stated that "Dr. Bratton must be returned to Canada...whether he is a criminal or not."

The Bratton abduction was discussed in the Canadian House of Commons. Edward Blake asked for information concerning the case, and expressed the indignation of all Canadians at this unparallelled outrage against a friendly nation. Prime Minister Sir John A. Macdonald replied that all the facts in connection with the kidnapping of Bratton had been forwarded to Sir Edward Thornton, British minister at Washington, and to the British Home Government. The Prime Minister stated that the Governor General had requested Sir Edward Thornton to make application to the United States government for the return of Dr. Bratton to Canada.

During this period of inter-governmental negotiations, rumour of war with the United States was prevalent in Ontario. It was said that Britain had threatened war if Dr. Bratton was not returned to Canada at once. Washington recognized the justness of the British protest, and the Canadians were assured that the United States government "will send him back to Canada without delay, and indemnify him for the arrest."

On June 15, 1872, Dr. Bratton returned to London a hero. He arrived in time to be a witness at the trial of one of his abductors, Isaac Bell Cornwall. Cornwall subsequently received three years in jail for his part in the kidnapping.

Dr. Bratton, this time under his own name, continued to practice medicine in London until 1877. When President Hayes took office, the Federal troops were withdrawn from South Carolina. Dr. Bratton was permitted to return to Yorkville, and no charges were ever brought against him.

The Bratton affair brought Joseph G. Hester some renown. He went to North Carolina where he teamed up with Albion Tourgee in hunting down Klansmen. Tourgee was a former Union army officer and former carpetbagger turned North Carolina Supreme Court judge. These two men led a concerted attack on the Ku Klux Klan in North Carolina.

Although in 1872 Western Ontario was practically defenseless because British troops had been withdrawn in 1869, the United States government did not want unfriendly relations with Canada. This was in the spirit of the 1871 Treaty of Washington in which the United States and Great Britain expressed a desire to settle all disputes between them by peaceful means. However, the Bratton case did show the United States government that the new Dominion of Canada was not afraid to stand up in defence of its integrity.

FORTS, FURS...AND HENS!

by Edna L. Lifeso

Can you imagine anyone transporting five ordinary chickens 2000 miles by canoe and portage from Montreal to the far-away valley of the North Saskatchewan River? You will say, "He must have been very fond of eggs," or "it could have been a bet of some kind."

Neither: the ambitious traveller was a canny Scot, and not given to such foolishness. Eggs he may have liked, but of greater importance was the unconscious longing to have something from the old land, from familiar boyhood days, in the lonely, turbulent life of a fur-trading post in Canada's new Northwest.

And so, a black hen, three speckled hens, and a rooster were finally able to put adventurous claws down on solid ground at the new Nor'West Company Post of Fort Vermilion in the fall of 1796. For the first time in the history of the Canadian prairies, the rising sun was welcomed by the clarion call of a rooster. The sound echoed and re-echoed between the high wooded hills where the swift-flowing Vermilion River is lost in the glacier-fed waters of the mighty North Saskatchewan.

Alexander Henry the Younger, son of the famous Henry the Elder, was able to write in his diary of January 4, 1797, "My black hen laid an egg today." How exciting such a simple event must have been!

The canoe-ferry, which Henry used in some of his fur-trading operations, has been replaced by the $800,000 Lea Park Bridge, a few miles north of Marwayne, Alberta. His "Great River" is part of a quiet scene of prosperous farm homes, peaceful, well-tilled fields and cattle grazing on the poplar bluffs. A gravelled highway winds down from the north, across the bridge, and up the farther hills toward Lloydminster, Edmonton, and then points south.

Just to the east of the bridge, on the north shore of the river, a high page-wire fence encloses a plot of ground containing a small poplar bluff. Almost hidden on the bluff is a gray cement shaft. This shaft marks the site of long abandoned Fort Vermilion, in 1794 the Western-most Post of either of Canada's great fur companies.

One marvels at the size of the poplars growing out of the many partly-filled pits that must have been cellars. One great, deep pit could only have been an ice-hole for storing fresh meat. One hundred years ago, the surrounding area was literally whitened with the bones of slaughtered buffalo. In imagination, one can almost feel the earth vibrate with the pounding of millions of hoofs.

Through Henry's journal, let us visit the site he chose in 1794, for a fur-trading post.

Axes swung rhythmically as bearded, red-sashed voyageurs felled spruce and poplar and lopped off the branches. Keeping time to some lusty French-Canadian boating song, other men of might rolled or carried the logs into a rough rectangular shape for the new palisade. Squaws tended pots slung over the heaped red embers of lazy cooking fires. Slinking dogs and innumerable dusky, half clad children played everywhere, all under the watchful stare of stoical red men. Fort Vermilion was under construction.

The culmination of the year's work was the trip to Fort William.

Alexander Henry the Younger had chosen the site for his company's new post carefully: a bench part way up the high north slope of the river. The broad "Theiscatchiwan" afforded some protection from the unpredictable Blackfoot who ranged the open country to the south. Situated at the confluence of the two rivers, the post commanded trade from all directions.

The new stockade was constructed from "good, stout, 15 foot logs standing on end"—according to Henry's diary. On the inside, 3½ feet down from the top, a walk of hewn planks afforded a "lookout", or a means of defence in case of an Indian attack.

Inside the walls, the main building was the trading post. There was also a large fur-shed, the factor's house, and at least ten "men's" houses. One wonders at the number of people required to carry on the work of the post. Henry's journal lists, besides the factor and his helper, 130 people—36 men, 27 women, and 67 children. Among the voyageurs the names of Parenteau, Dumont, Cardinal and Ladouceur bear witness to the ancestry of countless Metis families who are today scattered over the northern prairies.

All buildings were constructed of logs from the surrounding slopes. Cracks between the logs were chinked with moss or a special kind of clay that hardened and dried like cement. This clay was often mixed with chopped grass to give it greater adhesion. Glass windows were non-existent; transporting live chickens from Montreal was one thing, but glass presented much greater problems. Window openings were usually covered with pieces of deer-skin that had been scraped thin.

Frequently, trading posts of the two rival fur companies, Hudson Bay and Nor'West, were enclosed in the same palisade. Such was the case at Fort Vermilion. There seems to have been a minimum of friction, except perhaps, at the height of the trading season. Then, each factor was duty-bound to collect all the furs he could. However, tensions eased once again, with the end of trading.

The post was a beehive of activity throughout the year. With the warlike Blackfoot as neighbours, a surprise attack could be expected at any time, so the stockade had to be kept in good condition.

Alexander Henry was something of a gardener, as well as explorer and fur-trader. His diary of Oct. 6, 1796 furnished this surprising information: "Gathered all my turnips—about 50 bushels, very large and of excellent quality." What a welcome addition to a diet that was primarily meat of one kind or another!

Henry tells us that the Blackfoot had a buffalo-pound near the present town of Marwayne, so he could usually trade for whatever meat he needed at the fort. Much of this was made into pemmican; pounded to a pulp with stone hammers, and mixed with fat and berries—saskatoons or chokecherries preferably—the meat was then packed in skin bags of 50-90 pounds weight each. As many as 135 of these bags were filled by the squaws at Fort Vermilion every year.

Pemmican was used mainly on long trips. It had several advantages over fresh meat: it required no cooking, it was very nourishing, and it would keep for an indefinite period of time.

Not all of the meat was made into pemmican however. A surprising amount was frozen and used as fresh meat. A huge pit, lined with blocks of ice, could accomodate 700-800 buffalo carcasses. The heads and feet were removed, and the unskinned quarters were packed in more ice with a thick layer of hay spread over all. A shed protected it from the heat of the sun.

Travel was mostly by water, so a fleet of canoes, as well as the larger freight boats, had to be maintained at the Fort. Birch-bark to cover the framework, and gum to caulk the seams were collected by workers at the post or taken in trade from the Wood Crees to the north. But not all travel was by way of the rivers. Horses were taken in trade from the Blackfoot, and Henry maintained a sizeable herd. Some were kept near the fort, but the main band was kept in the vicinity of the present town of Elk Point, Alberta. The horses were used in cross-country travel to different Indian camps, by hunting parties, for hauling fire-wood and hay, and for various other chores around the fort.

The broad "Theiscatchiwan" afforded some protection from the unpredictable Blackfoot.

The culmination of the year's work—and something eagerly looked forward to by those lucky enough to go—was the trip to Fort William in the spring with the winter's accumulation of furs. In 1809. Henry's party left Fort Vermilion on May 10th, as soon as rivers and lakes were free of ice. To allow more room for the furs, which had been pressed into bales weighing about 90 lbs. each, the heavily laden canoes carried barely enough food to last to the next supply station. That was Fort a la Corne near the present city of Prince Albert. There, supplies of pemmican, corn, wild rice, and other foodstuffs were taken on to last to the next station, near the Pas.

At each Nor'West post along the route, Henry's party was augmented by another fleet of fur-canoes heading for the same destination. The old route of the fur-traders followed the Saskatchewan River through all its tortuous length to the point where it empties into Lake Winnipeg. From Fort Maurepas at the head of the lake, the route followed the short Winnipeg River, then portaged over the height of land to Lake of the Woods, and on to Lake Superior, the world's largest body of fresh water.

The singing, quick-tempered, hard-paddling voyageurs reached Fort William on June 18. They had covered a distance of 1750 miles, at an average of nearly 45 miles a day.

The month spent at Fort William, "half-way house" of the North West Fur Company, was the one "break" for the prairie dwellers in the whole busy year. Then the partners from Montreal met their partners from the lonely scattered posts of the far north-west, giving the latter a chance to receive messages from home and to catch up on the news of the day. The partners discussed company affairs, division of the proceeds from the previous year's furs, establishment of new posts and the possible abandonment of old ones. For the Metis and Indian canoe-men, it was a time to dance and sing, to drink and fight, to gamble and to tell stories, to have fun.

Then the summer partners—"the pork-eaters"—returned to Montreal with canoe-loads of furs for European markets. The winter partners—"the fat-eaters"—loaded their canoes with a maximum of trade goods and a minimum of food, and returned to the prairies. As on the way out, food stores were replenished at each station along the way.

The crew of each canoe—5 men and one woman—consumed about 3 bushels of corn, 3 bushels of wild rice, 25 lbs of grease, and 540 lbs of pemmican on the two-way trip, according to Henry's diary. He wrote, "I arrived at Fort Vermilion on Sept. 13 with a brigade of 11 canoes, carrying 28 pieces each." A piece weighed about 90 lbs., so each canoe carried close to 2500 lbs. of trade goods.

Soon after his return, Henry found 300 Blackfoot tepees pitched on the west shore of the Vermilion River. Unused to river travel, the visiting Indians had to be ferried across the Saskatchewan to the trading post. Because of their warlike nature, only three were taken across each trip.

Gifts of rum and tobacco preceded the business of trading. "We do not make our liquor so strong for the Blackfoot," Henry tells us. "A 9 gal. keg of liquor contains 4-5 qts. of high wine, and the rest is water. For Crees and Assiniboines, we put in 6 qts. of wine, for the Saulteaus, 8-9 qts." Evidently, care was taken to avoid upsetting the hair-trigger tempers of the Blackfoot.

The return of the fur brigade was properly celebrated. "We had a dance at my house to which we invited the Hudson Bay man and his family. But we were much crowded, there being present 72 men, 37 women, and 65 children in a room 22 by 23 ft. making it disagreeably warm."

Fort Vermilion was abandoned in 1810. Henry's journal reads. "We mounted and abandoned the post, leaving the ice-house open. The building contained 400 limbs of buffalo, still frozen."

* * * *

The picture fades, and once more, we are aware of the great steel structure that spans Henry's "Theiscatchewan" River where his canoe-ferry used to ply. Before we return completely to the present, we take one last look at the weed-filled hollows that once were cellars, and the slim gray shaft that marks the site of almost forgotten Fort Vermilion, Nor'West post of Alexander Henry the Younger in 1794.

THE BATTLE OF LUNDY'S LANE
by Tom Arnett

A description of the historic battle of Lundy's Lane reads like the brainchild of an inexperienced but highly imaginative television script assistant—lots of action but completely unbelievable. Yet to the 2,800 British and Canadian and the 4,000 American troops who clashed on the evening of July 25th, 1814, it was quite real: so real hundreds of them lost their lives and many more were wounded and/or taken prisoner.

Lundy's Lane, fought on the heights near Niagara Falls, Ontario, was one of the final battles of the War of 1812.

The war itself had grown out of a number of irritations rather than one clear-cut issue. The American states had won their independence from Great Britain more than a quarter-century earlier—36 years earlier, to be exact, although peace settlements had dragged on for years.

Loyalists had fled to Canada where they could start new lives but remain under British rule. The "plain folk"—Quakers, Amish and Mennonites—led the exodus.

Then, as the new republic found its feet and got a grasp on prosperity, a small trickle of migration started to go the other way. British seamen in particular, doomed to the life of drudgery serving under officers who got their commissions through

Desertion became the rule.

the pull of wealth and an old family name, saw the United States as a country where a young man could get ahead. Desertion became the rule as discontented British seamen decided to "have a go" on an American vessel where wages were higher and the chances of advancement much better.

Britain, still smarting from the loss of her colonies, was loath to suffer in silence through such further affronts. What to do?—Why, stop American vessels on the high seas and search for these deserters.

Now the American powers became indignant. Fuel for the fires came in the form of suspicions that Great Britain was trying to stir up the Western Indians to attack the U.S.

Overseas, Britain and much of Europe was engaged in the Napoleonic wars. This, for the British naval powers, meant the blockading of many European ports. U.S. ships crossed the Atlantic only to find the U.K. blockades between them and the European cities with which they hoped to trade. The young nation would endure many things but interference with commerce was not—and still isn't—one of them. On the 12th of June, 1812, the United States declared war.

On the 12th of June, 1812, the United States declared war.

Communications being somewhat slow, it was nearly two weeks later before Canadians heard rumors that there was a war on and their country was to be the battlefield. On June 29th, police in Quebec posted a notice that "authentic intelligence has been received that the Government of the United States of America did, on the 18th instant, declare war against the United Kingdom of Great Britain and Ireland and its dependencies...."

Those "dependencies" meant Canada. Since England was engaged in virtually a life-or-death struggle with Napoleon, she had little time or resources to spare for another round with her former colonies.

John Graves Simcoe, lieutenant-governor of Upper Canada, had to convince the British Government that Canada should be defended and came up with some theories on how this might be done. He pleaded for a naval force on the Great Lakes as "the cheapest mode of defence." Given his lead, Simcoe and his officers set to work. Volunteers were recruited, organized into militia battalions and taught to behave like soldiers and sailors. Every effort was made to win over the Indians to the British side and the few regular troops which were available were assembled at strategic spots.

Although the U.S. forces had an enormous edge in numbers of men and guns, the war dragged wearily on, partly, it is believed, because the American people were divided in opinion on the value of the war and, partly, due to the wholeheartedness with which Simcoe, Drummond, Brock, Prevost and other Canadian officers pursued the defence of their country.

Battle followed battle for two years. Desertion remained a major problem for the Canadians. In 1806 Colonel Isaac Brock had written:

"The lures to desertion continually thrown out by the Americans, and the facility with which it can be accomplished, exacting a more than ordinary precaution on the part of the officers, insensibly produce mistrust between them and the men, highly

"...the opposite shore is chiefly inhabited by the vilest characters."

prejudicial to the service. ... the opposite shore is chiefly inhabited by the vilest characters, who have an interest in debauching the soldier from his duty; since roads are open into the interior of the States which facilitate desertion, it is impossible to avoid the contagion."

The situation was much the same throughout the war and after many battles the list of missing

Sacketts Harbour, as drawn on the spot in 1812 by a British Army Officer.

included deserters as well as those taken prisoner.

The navy Simcoe wanted for the Lakes got its first taste of war in an engagement against the enemy at Sacketts Harbor on Lake Ontario. Here, so the story goes, the full Canadian force sailed against one U.S. ship armed with a 32 pounder long gun but no ammunition. The Canadians obligingly fired their 32 pounder, the Americans retrieved the ball, put it in their own gun and fired it back, virtually wiping out the Canadian flagship.

Win some, lose some—this is how the war progressed. General Brock took Detroit, but was killed at Queenston Heights. The Americans, with 4,000 troops at Sacketts Harbor and another 3,000 at Buffalo, proceeded to pillage and burn much of the Niagara Penninsula. Then, in the closing months of 1813, the British under Prevost and Major General Phineas Riall, a short, stout Irishman and a competent soldier, not only recaptured the Niagara frontier but, on New Years' day, 1814, left Buffalo a smoking ruin.

Rough, ready and pugnacious, Riall next marched his force into the Battle of Chippeaw on July 5, 1814. His summary defeat cut his troop of 2,000 men by at least a third and, in retreat, he was closely pursued by the Americans.

Sir Gordon Drummond, Riall's superior, was on the march from York with a few British regulars and a scattering of Canadian militia; he joined Riall and their combined force was about 2,800. Determined not to accept defeat, as Riall was about to do (he ordered his men to retreat from the area),

Drummond countermanded the order, and Riall's men, backed by Drummond's, were to encounter the Americans again.

The engagement came on July 25th, on a small hill at the junction of the river road opposite Niagara Falls and Lundy's Lane.

The Americans, in three brigades, were commanded by Major-General Brown and Generals Scott, Porter and Ripley. Brown, an officer from the New York Militia, was said to have so little military knowledge that he was unable to correctly post the guards when the regiment was in camp.

Scott, however, was a professional soldier, and "one of the most talented and best trained officers in the U.S. Army." Most of his hand-picked field officers were up to the same standard.

Porter was a congressman turned soldier, and had been one of the chief promoters of the war. Ripley, too was a politician, and had been a speaker in the Massachusetts assembly.

Under these assorted U.S. officers was a well-trained, well-equipped force of 4,000 men. Opposing them, at the top of the hill, were less than 3,000 assorted British regulars, Indians, Canadian farmers and boys.

The Americans retrieved the ball, put it in their own gun and fired it.

The recent rousting at Chippeaw had merely added to Riall's long list of troubles. His men were short of supplies—both food and arms—and without adequate clothing. The men had not been paid for six months; the desertion rate was high and morale could scarcely be at a lower point.

E. Cruikshank, writing in 1888, quotes documents to show that Riall's men were "so enfeebled by disease, exposure, and fatigue...that they had really become unfit for active service....nearly every man in (the regiment) had been down with dysentery or intermittant fever." As well, Cruikshank writes, "both in the Second Battalion of the 41st and the 103rd there were several companies of mere boys and the majority of both corps were so youthful that they had been retained in garrison during the whole of the previous year."

The signing of the treaty of peace at the end of the War of 1812.

Riall himself, although he had been an officer for twenty years, had seen little actual warfare. Supposedly, he was "short, stout, nearsighted, impetuously tempered, rashly brave."

Sick, discouraged, malnourished youths led by such a man should have been mere cannon fodder to Scott and his professional troops.

"The declining sun shone bright and cloudless," R.W. Geary's account puts it, "as troops of the opposing armies, with drums beating and colors flying, marched gallantly to their positions in the field." The declared intention of the American commander, writes Cruikshank, was to force his way by the shortest route to Burlington Heights where he expected to be met the next day by a squadron from Sacketts Harbour. The British and Canadians were taking a stand rather than yield a choice position.

Drummond's British "regulars" of the 89th regiment, the 8th Kings and the Royal Scots had the top of the hill, with their 24-pounder brass field guns in a nice line behind an old snake-rail fence. The 41st, 103rd, 104th, the Glengarry light troops and the Canadian militia helped to extend the British line in a crescent-shaped formation. A small group of pro-British Indians were stationed to the end of the crescent.

At some time between five-thirty and seven o'clock (accounts vary), the Americans charged the hill, directing their attack chiefly against the center and left of the British lines.

A British officer rode into American ranks and was taken prisoner.

A volley or two of grape shot answered the charge, but the Americans, momentarily stopped, rebounded quickly and charged again and again, eventually pushing Riall's force back a bit. The Glengarry division, fighting from among cherry and pear trees, was able to hold its own, but the Americans were soon gaining an advantage at the other end of the British/Canadian line.

Scott—perhaps having more military skills at his command than the battle really called for—decided, for variety, to send his 25th U.S. Infantry around, through some undergrowth, to attack the British from the rear.

Near darkness—for now it was about nine o'clock—contributed a measure to the confusion. So did the unexpected discovery by the British that a green uniform doesn't make a man an American.

Unaware that the Americans were behind as well as in front of them, a British officer, Captain Loring, rode into the American ranks and was taken prisoner. Later Riall himself was wounded and when his officers attempted to carry him from the field of battle they chose the same unfortunate route. Yelling "Make way for General Riall" they marched into the arms of the 25th Infantry, where they were joyfully received.

The loud cheering that followed this easy capture of the British general, however, alerted Drummond to the situation and brought a rain of shot down on the 25th.

Smoke and haze from the guns, plus darkness and the small dimensions of the battle area all contributed to the confusion. The combatants were, at times, within yards of one another.

Under the shield of darkness, some 1,400 U.S. troops armed with bayonets crept up the hill towards the rail fence, unobserved by the British gunners who were occupied with firing on the U.S. batteries at the foot of the hill. Under cover of the fence, the Americans fired, from close range, at the British gunners. Then, leaping the fence, they were able to take virtually all the British heavy artillery simultaneously. Any British gunners who had survived the fire from the fence row were immediately bayonetted.

Taking advantage of this distraction—for losing their gunners and guns did distract the British—another U.S. brigade, led by Ripley, advanced up the hill. At this close range the Americans, who had three large buck shot as well as regular bullets in their cartridges, were able to inflict further severe losses on the British.

The fierceness and determination of the remaining British and Canadian forces, however, was far greater than anyone (especially the Americans) would have expected. The hill was now a scene of chaos. Fighting was often hand to hand, with soldiers using their musket butts as clubs. Scott decided to advance his howitzer to the hill but on nearing the fray, the men in charge of it were shot. The horses, terrified and confused, continued the haul until the gun was gratefully received by British hands.

The next day Drummond had to explain it all in his official report, or dispatch. In what was a masterpiece of literary diplomacy, he wrote:

"The darkness of the night, during this extraordinary conflict, occasioned several uncommon incidents: our troops having for a moment been pushed back, some of our guns remained for a few minutes in the enemy's hands; they were, however, not only quickly recovered, but the two pieces, a sixpounder, and a five and a half inch howitzer, which the enemy had brought up, were captured by us, together with several tumbrils; and in limbering up our guns, at one period, one of the enemy's sixpounders was put by mistake upon a limber of ours, and one of our six-pounders limbered on one of his, by which means the pieces were exchanged; and thus though we captured two of his guns, yet as he obtained one of ours, we have gained only one gun."

On the other side, Brigadier-General Winfield Scott, having had two horses killed from under him, was eventually wounded and had to be carried off the field. Porter was wounded and General Brown was also shot, first in the thigh and then in the side. Ripley, who at this time had merely had a shot go through his hat, was given the U.S. command.

Major Riddle's sketch of the battle, July 25, 1814, engraved by W. Strickland.

On the British side, Drummond was down, his horse dead and himself with a wound in the neck. Riall was wounded and captured. Morrison, field officer of the 89th regiment, was wounded as was the officer in charge of the Royals and both Lieutenant Colonel Robertson of the militia and the chief of the 104th.

The fighting continued until midnight, or, as one early report says, "They fought until they could fight no more." In his after-the-fact dispatch, Drummond was to state that his men conducted themselves "with the most perfect steadiness and intrepid gallantry, and the enemy was constantly repulsed with heavy loss."

The Americans, with nearly one third of their men either dead or wounded, then retreated three miles to the Chippawa, leaving the British in possession of the hill and a considerable number of dead or wounded American troops.

The British kept up their fire as Ripley retreated, but were too beat to pursue the enemy as it withdrew. They, too, had lost nearly one-third of their total number. Their main regiment, the 89th,

lost 254 men out of a total of 400; the Royals lost some 200 (out of 500). In all, they reported 876 officers and men killed, wounded or missing.

The surviving British Light troops and some Indians were dispatched in pursuit but these soon returned (with a few prisoners), feeling too weakened to attempt another full-scale encounter.

Technically, neither side won the Battle of Lundy's Lane but that the British held the hill and the Americans withdrew in "an attempt of retreat" is as much as most of us need to know. The U.S. invasion of Upper Canada had been checked and the American army's role changed from that of aggression to one of defence.

To quote R.W. Geary, president of the Lundy's Lane Historical Society in 1914 when the centennial of the battle was celebrated: Lundy's Lane was "the last fight of the last campaign of the last war between the United States and the United Kingdom. ...It is one of the few critical battles in history in which both armies were victorious, and both were defeated."

SLUMACH'S GLORIOUS GOLD

BRITISH COLUMBIA'S FAMOUS LOST MINE

by Brian Antonson

This photo is purported to be of Slumach, but the real Slumach was advanced in years, and this photo of a young man would have been taken years before photography was developed.

$100,000,000 in GOLD—waiting to be picked up:at the once-stable price of $35 an ounce, that's what British Columbia's fabled Lost Creek Gold Mine has been said to be worth, and now—well, the finder could vie for the title of world's richest man.

The Lost Creek Gold Mine story centres around a Salish Indian named Slumach who lived and died in the late 1800's. It has all of the elements of an intriguing lost-treasure story: murder, a gallows-curse, a list, at least 25 names long, of people who have fallen victim to the curse, and yearly expeditions by the gold-hungry who search for the lost motherlode.

The story begins with a legend that research has shown is largely false, but somewhere in there some truth appears. In 1972, my brother, a friend and myself researched and published a short book dealing with the facts and fantasies behind the Lost Creek Mine. We found an incredibly tangled web of differing tales that conflicted, confused, and in some cases substantiated each other, but finally a thin line of truth began to emerge, and what we wound up with was almost as baffling as what we had started with: it appears that the gold just might really be there, but the Indian Slumach never had anything to do with it!

Let's look at the legend: the story goes that Slumach showed up in New Westminster one night in 1889 and threw a handful of gold nuggets across a barroom floor. He refused to reveal the source of his booty, and when he finally left town a few days later, he was followed by citizens looking for easy riches. But the wily Slumach evaded his followers and disappeared into the rough country near Pitt Lake, some twenty miles from New Westminster.

Some time later, Slumach reappeared with more nuggets in his possession. When he left this time, he took a young Indian girl with him to help with his cooking. Again, he eluded his trackers and disappeared into the deep bush without a trace. Slumach returned some months later, but the Indian

girl was never seen again. The Indian claimed she had left him on the way to his secret mine and he hadn't seen her since.

Over a period of fourteen months, Slumach made eight trips into the rugged Pitt Lake country, each time successfully evading those who tried to follow him. And each time he took a young woman with him; none of them were ever seen alive again.

Slumach threw a handful of gold nuggets across the barroom floor.

About here, a police constable named Eric Granger comes into the picture; it was Granger's assigned task to investigate the mysterious disappearances of the young women who had left with Slumach.

In the summer of 1890, a young Irish-Chinese girl named Molly Tynan arrived in New Westminster, swearing she would master the Indian Slumach and share his wealth. Granger tried to stop her but she left with Slumach on his next trip, and they disappeared into the wilds. A short time later, a fisherman working on the Fraser River pulled her body up in his nets. This time, there was no mistaking what had happened—Slumach's knife was still in her heart.

When Slumach returned to New Westminster he was arrested, tried and convicted of Molly's murder. Refusing to reveal the location of his secret mine, he went to his death on the gallows with a bitter curse: "Nika memloose, mine memloose"— "When I die, mine dies."

Ten years after Slumach's death in 1891, an Alaskan prospector named John Jackson stopped in New Westminster on his way to San Francisco and picked up the legend of Slumach's mine. He embarked on a search, swearing to stay in the bush until he had found the gold. In the fall of 1901, he

The Indian girl was never seen again.

stumbled out of the bush—a weak and broken man. He refused to allow anyone near his packsack, which seemed unusually heavy, and a few days later left New Westminster. Later, reports came back from San Francisco that he had deposited $8000 in raw gold with the Bank of British North America (later the Bank of Montreal.) Unfortunately, this important piece of evidence can never be confirmed, because a few year's later, Jackson's bank was destroyed by fire (possibly in the earthquake of 1906) and all records of any deposit he might have made were lost.

At this point, Jackson made the most significant contribution of anyone to the legend: he wrote a letter. The hardships he had endured in his hunt for the gold had ruined his health, and in San Francisco, he became bedridden. Knowing he was dying, he wrote a letter to a Seattle friend named Shotwell, who had grubstaked him on earlier expeditions. In his letter, Jackson described how

Did these girls fall victim to Slumach's evil ways?

91

Sheridan Hill sports an old mine shaft thought at one time to lead to Slumach's gold.

Shotwell might find the mine, and said of it, "Don't give up...and you will be repaid beyond your wildest dreams." But Shotwell wasn't interested in hunting for the mine himself. Instead, he made copies of the letter and sold them. Jackson died in 1904 without ever hearing of his mine again.

Since that time, perhaps as many as 36 people have died in the hunt for Slumach's Lost Creek Gold Mine. Each death heaped more suspicion on the "cursed" mine. The latest recorded death was that of Louis Hagbo of Bremerton, Washington, in 1963. Hagbo went into the bush on a hunt for the mine,

"Nika memloose, mine memloose"—
"When I die, mine dies."

and when he didn't return as scheduled, his son-in-law went in after him. He found Hagbo's body at the bottom of a cliff—he had apparently suffered a heart attack while attempting to scale the rock-face. The local press carried the story under the headline "LOST MINE'S 23rd VICTIM."

So much for the legend—now, where in all of this does the truth lie? First off, the Indian Slumach did die on the gallows at New Westminster's Provincial Gaol (jail) in 1891—but not for the murder of Molly Tynan. In fact, nobody's sure if Molly Tynan ever existed. And there's no record of a Constable Granger either. But this much is true: Slumach did

commit at least one murder. On September 8, 1890, he shot a half-breed Kanaka (Indians of mixed Hawaiian blood) named Louis Bee, at a slough near Pitt Lake. He disappeared into the bush and led authorities on an exhausting chase for over two months until starvation and the approach of winter finally forced him to surrender. He was tried in November, found guilty and sentenced to die on January 16, 1891. The BRITISH COLUMBIAN newspaper edition for that date notes. "Old Slumach was hanged in the yard of the provincial gaol this morning at 8 o'clock for the murder on September 8th last, of Louis Bee, a half-breed."

In our research for our book, we scrutinized the Bench Book kept by Mr. Justice Drake, the judge who presided over Slumach's trial. There was no mention whatsoever of gold. Witnesses stated how they feared Slumach, and noted that he was known to be violent and mysterious, but there is not one single mention of gold. In fact, there is no mention of Slumach's supposed exploits in New Westminster's bars in any newspaper of the day. It seems highly unlikely that the journalists of early New Westminster and Vancouver would miss a story of a man repeatedly throwing around gold nuggets. Yet, though there seems to be nothing to support any kind of a legend, there was enough of a story circulating to capture the interest of John Jackson when he arrived in New Westminster in 1901.

No one has ever tried to determine if John Jackson really did exist, because Jackson was apparently quite well-known at the time and there was never any question about him. As for his legendary gold findings, we've already mentioned the bank fire that destroyed any bank records that could substantiate that. The letter to Shotwell has shown up in so many different hands that there is no way of knowing for sure whether Jackson actually wrote it. Still, the Jackson incident is probably the most reliable part of the whole lost mine story.

"Don't give up...and you will be repaid beyond your wildest dreams."

In his letter, Jackson makes several references to mining terms that only a prospector would be familiar with, and according to experts his descriptions are completely authentic. Also, the earliest recorded stories of the mine appear in 1906 newspapers, containing tales of people who have died under the mine's curse, and one such story tells of Jackson.

As I mentioned earlier, a number of people have been lost while hunting for the mine—each one adding to the belief that Slumach's curse is working. One of the most famous people to disappear while searching for the gold was R.A. "Volcanic" Brown. Brown was well known throughout British Columbia as a prospector, having established several mines, some of which are still in operation today. He began searching for Slumach's lost gold in 1923 and searched every year until 1930. In 1929 he turned back from his journey into the Pitt Lake mountains when he missed the campfire smoke of some people he had found were following him. He discovered one of the men injured on the trail and helped him back to civilization. This gallant gesture put Brown behind schedule and he was caught by the early snows in the mountains. A search team was sent out when he failed to return on time and he was rescued, but not before he had cut off several of his toes with a hunting knife after they had been frozen.

A year later he returned to the mountains and was never seen again. A search team, including two RCMP officers, moved into the country in late November. Members of the team found Brown's last camp high on the Stave Glacier, his coffee-pot still on the fire grate and all of his belongings left just as if he had stepped out of camp for only a moment. They surmised he might have walked away in a snowstorm and fallen down a crevasse.

The most intriguing thing about Brown's disappearance was found amongst his belongings in his tent: a glass jar containing 11 ounces of raw gold that had been chipped out of a vein.

There are others who have died or disappeared while searching for the mine. In the early fifties a prospector named Alfred Gaspard set up an elaborate base-camp system, complete with a radio link to the outside world, and began a systematic exploration of the valleys in the area where he

The most intriguing thing about Brown's disappearance: a glass jar containing 11 ounces of raw gold— found in his tent.

thought the mine to be. He reported daily on his progress, and at one point said that he felt he was closing in on the mine. A few days later he missed his radio rendezvous. A search, partially paid for by an emergency fund he had set up, failed to find any sign of Gaspard, and he became but another name on the list of curse victims.

In the late sixties, a Port Moody, British Columbia janitor named Tiny Allen bragged to a *Columbian* newspaper reporter that he would dump a sack full of gold on the reporter's desk when he found the mine. Some time later he called to say that he had just returned from a trip into the mountains, and had seen the mine from a ledge above it. He

Mountains north and east of Pitt Lake, said to hold the long-sought "glory-hole" found by Jackson, Brown and Allen.

described the scene to the reporter who then asked if he had ever read Jackson's letter. Allen replied that he hadn't—and that's interesting because he had just described to the reporter a strange pyramid-shaped rock, with its top cut off that he had seen on the valley floor. Jackson's letter tells of how he buried some gold beneath a "large tent shaped rock...there is a mark cut out in it." The two descriptions were too close to be coincidental. But as with so many others, tragedy struck Tiny Allen—he died of a heart attack before he could return to the mine site.

In our research, we talked to many people who had had experiences relating to the mine. Just a few months ago, I received a phone call from an eighty-year-old man who had just read our book and wanted to tell us that he had been with his father and some Indian guides many years before on a trip up Pitt Lake to a point near the mine. Like many others, his supposed location was just another possibility.

The bedrock runs yellow with raw gold and nuggets the size of walnuts can be picked up off the ground.

There are at least a half-dozen popular locations for the lost gold. One is near Widgeon Creek, which flows into the Pitt River just above the point where the Pitt joins the Fraser. This location would put the mine within easy reach of frontier New Westminster, but since the area is fairly well travelled by hikers, it's not likely that such a bonanza would be missed.

Another possibility is Sheridan Hill, a rocky outcropping that was once looked on as a holy place by Indians. Sheridan Hill is located near Pitt Lake's southern shore and is quite accessible to Sunday drivers who often drop by just to see. In 1961, the Hill figured in a series of newspaper articles brought about by a dream—a former prospector

had dreamt the gold was to be found in the Hill. Sure enough, an investigating team found a mine shaft on the hillside but no gold was ever located. For weeks though, the area was crowded with gold-seekers and curious spectators.

Some other locations on the shores of Pitt Lake have been the subject of searches over the years, but the most likely location is at the headwaters of Corbold Creek, high in the mountains to the north-east of the lake. This would be near Volcanic Brown's last camp, and in the area where both Jackson and Tiny Allen claimed to have stumbled on the gold. This area is extremely dangerous and trying—subject to landslides and sudden dense fog. (In 1958, an American television crew went into the area on a filming jaunt for a series on lost hordes called "Treasure." They reached the area where Indian guides told them the mine was supposed to be, but when they moved closer to the site, ground fog moved in and stayed for three days. They ran out of food and finally had to move out without going any further.

If indeed the mine exists, it's worth could be astronomical at today's prices for the precious yellow metal. According to the stories, the mine is a "glory-hole," where the bedrock runs yellow with raw gold and nuggets the size of walnuts can be picked up off the ground.

One very important note: this article is not intended to breed a rush of gold seekers heading for Pitt Lake. Rather, it recounts the known facts about an interesting legend. The Pitt Lake country has been described as "some of the worst topographical area in the province," and that's just what it is—incredibly steep and rugged, accessible only on foot, and terribly dangerous for even experienced bushmen. Yet every year, Lower Mainland libraries and newspapers are deluged with requests for information about the mine from would-be billionaires. But Slumach's supposed secret still lies safe, deep in the foreboding mountains—and poor Slumach must be laughing in his grave, because it's not even his fault! ⊕

New Westminster in the late 1800's—Slumach's time.

CHARLES M. RUSSELL
The Year In Canada

by John W. Chalmers

As Charlie Russell's deft fingers modeled the beautiful buck antelope, no doubt the artist was recalling how he had been given the pronghorn's Blackfoot name, Ah-Wah-Cous, or "trotter." That could have been a romantic incident, resulting from appreciation by the Indian chief, Medicine Whip, of Russell's grace, speed, or virile good looks. Alas, it was none of these. When the Blood (or Kainai) chieftain first met the wandering cowboy, the latter was wearing a pair of threadbare jeans or trousers, the seat of which was patched with buckskin. To the

imaginative Bloods, it resembled nothing so much as "the north end of an antelope going south," as two biographers have delicately expressed it.

The incident occurred during Russell's Canadian year, from May, 1888, to March, 1889. Despite the fact that this sojourn in what is now Southern Alberta seems to have had a profound effect on his career and his life, so little hard information about this period survives that at least one writer has designated it as his "lost" or "forgotten" year. Undeterred by the lack of factual material, others

"When Law Dulls the Edge of Chance."

"Single-Handed"

seem to have drawn heavily on their imaginations to supply such deficiencies. Thus, one scribe has Russell first communicating with the Bloods through the sign language, in which he was highly proficient, another states that he "could use the sign language well enough to get along," and a third source states he learned it in Canada. Some authors suggest—others categorically affirm—the existence of a rather torrid romance between Russell and a Blood maiden called Keeoma. Neither Russell nor his wife, understandably, ever admitted such a romantic involvement; nor did they explicitly deny it. If the story was a myth, it at least was good for business.

All writers have assumed, probably correctly, that Russell spent the entire 1888-89 winter on the Blood reserve, and one devotes an entire chapter to this period. Yet the Blood Indian Agency's record of long-term activities, very carefully kept at that period, reveals no trace of this important sojourner.

Perhaps some of the uncertainty about Russell's life at the period under discussion arises from indiscriminate use of such terms as Blood (or Kainai, as noted), Blackfoot, and Piegan (Canadian spelling Peigan). All of these peoples are Blackfoot-speakers. Today they consist of four bands, the Blackfoot proper (note Canadian use of singular form), east of Calgary, the Peigans, west of Fort

Macleod, the Blood, south of Fort Macleod and Lethbridge, and the Blackfeet, near Browning. The latter, and indeed the whole group, have often been referred to as Piegans.

To the imaginative Bloods, it resembled "the north end of an antelope going south."

Returning now to the future Ah-Wah-Cous, it seems that he left Helena on May 16, 1888, in the company of his friends Phil Weinard, "Long Green" Stillwell, and another cowboy, J. Green. Apparently twenty-four-year old Weinard had just married the niece of Mrs. "Chicago Joe" Hensley, manager of the Coliseum Theatre, an alliance which that lady thoroughly disapproved of. To avoid her wrath, Weinard shipped his bride east and with his disreputable friends, he fled to his High River homestead in the District of Alberta, N.W.T. After all the spring round-up was over, and perhaps there was little work available, so the northern excursion appealed to the footloose cowpunchers.

Shortly after crossing the Forty-Ninth Parallel, Russell had his first encounter with the famed Mounties. His friend Billy Henry tells of the incident:

I remember Charlie telling how he saw some Mounties and Indians while coming up to High River. They were in a line on the trail. In the lead was a Mountie followed by three Indian prisoners and another Mountie taking up the rear. Charlie was very impressed with this sight and when he got to the shack he made a painting of it. I don't know what became of it. This is the only Russell picture definitely known to have been painted in Canada. Russell presented it to his future host, Charlie Blount (or Blunt). It was Russell's first Mounted Police work.

Green soon dropped out of the party, perhaps even before reaching the Canadian border. The now-married Weinard returned to his own home. Stillwell spent the summer with Russell but returned to Montana in September.

Somerton was cleaning his gun and found it ornamented with two beautifully executed etchings.

Soon after crossing into Canada, the Americans met Charlie Blount, an amateur artist. The two Charlies immediately took to each other, with the result that Russell and Stillwell spent the summer in a little cabin on the Highwood, about six miles from the settlement of High River. Authorities differ as to whether they were (free) tenants of a previously-empty building or Blount's house guests. In any event, they passed a pleasant summer, fishing, perhaps doing a little hunting, soaking up scenery and atmosphere, and, for Russell, no doubt painting and drawing. Since Blount was a close friend of the Canadian cattleman George Lane, it is probable he introduced Russell and Lane to each other, then or later, beginning a relationship that was to prove

richly rewarding, financially and otherwise, to the cowboy artist.

Apparently no art medium was beyond Russell's ken, as the following story indicates:

One glorious day in the fall of '88 a small party of which the writer was a member left High River for a big hill on the north side of the river, west of the crossing, in search of antelope. The party, with others, included the late W.H. Somerton and Chas. Russell.

During the day a halt was made for lunch and during the smoke hour that followed, Russell picked up Somerton's rifle and unnoticed, occupied himself with etching on the side plates with the sharp point of a knife. This passed unobserved until the next day, when Somerton was cleaning his gun and found it was ornamented with two beautifully executed etchings. On one side an old bull buffalo, evidently at his last stand with a coyote patiently waiting for the coming feast. On the reverse appeared an Indian, holding his cayuse, and mournfully regarding two buffalo heads in the grass.

In September, 1888, Russell and Stillwell headed south to Montana. Enroute, Russell accepted an invitation to visit the Blood reserve. One authority states that the invitation came from young Sleeping Thunder, who was (or was not) the son of a sub-chief named Medicine Whip and who became a close friend of the artist. Another, however, suggests that it was Chief Black Eagle who urged the migrant to stay. But Dr. Hugh A. Dempsey, Director of History at the Glenbow-Alberta Institute in Calgary, and an authority on the Blackfoot people, states that such names as Sleeping Thunder, Medicine Whip and Keeoma are all unknown to the Bloods although a Thunder Chief was head chief.

"Canadian Mounted Police with Prisiners" [sic]

Black Eagle was a common Blood name, but not borne by any chief.

However, there is little doubt that Russell remained with the Bloods until the following March. In any event, he got to know them so well that his portrayal of Indians ever after was influenced by his stay with them. For instance, one Blood friend told Russell the coup-counting story which the artist later depicted in "When Sioux and Blackfeet Meet."

The same man taught Russell much. For example:

> We make sacrifices to the Great Spirit. You've seen us place our best blankets, a scarlet cloth, or the skin of some animal upon a pole or medicine lodge to be left there, never to be touched again. Then we have our Sun Dance as part of our worship. When we smoke, that is worship, too. Our tobacco and kinnickinnick are sacred.

It was perhaps this lesson which inspired the bronze "Smoke of the Medicine Man" in 1923.

The Bloods apparently urged Russell to marry one of their girls and stay with them. This fact (if it so is) and Russell's three Keeoma pictures (one of his wife) have led some biographers to infer, and others to state, that Russell and Keeoma were sweethearts and came close to effecting an enduring union. Such romantics have been misled; Keeoma, or Kee-O-Mee, is not a proper noun. According to one authority, it, or rather "akeeoma," is a Blackfoot word meaning "she's married."

In March, 1889, Russell headed back to Montana, little more affluent than when he left, but enriched in experience and understanding that were to provide artistic capital for the rest of his life. Such Canadian-inspired works include "Peace Talk" (1890), "Inside the Lodge" (1893), "Squaw Travois" (1895), the three "Keeomas" (1896-98), "Three Generations," and "On the Move" (1903). Among his bronzes are "Sign Talk," possibly a likeness of Russell's Cree friend Young Man, "Blood Brother"

The Mounties fascinated him.

(1900), "Offering to the Sun Gods" (1902), "Piegan Maiden" (1902), and "Medicine Whip," (1911) perhaps a Blood named Heavily Whipped. Others are "The Robe Flesher" (1925), "Blackfoot War Dance" (1928), "Blackfoot War Chief," and no doubt many more. "In the White Man's World" depicts the Cree Young Boy as a buffalo horn-pedlar, but it is not sure whether Russell met him in Canada or in Montana.

His Canadian experience also provided him with another range of subjects, the North West Mounted Police. Probably no single artist has contributed more to the popular image of that peculiarly

"The Queen's War Hounds"

Canadian institution than has the American Charlie Russell. The Mounties fascinated him almost as much as did the Montana cowpunchers, the Blackfoot Indians, and the mountain men. He came back to the Force time after time, long after his 1889 return to Montana. His NWMP pictures include "Canadian Mounted Police Bringing in Red Prisiners" (sic) 1888), "The Talk Paper" (1902), "Single-Handed" (1912), "Caught with the Goods" (1913), "The Queen's War Hounds" (1914), "When Law Dulls the Edge of Chance" (1915). Stetsoned Mounties also appear on an undated letter to Ralph Kendall and on the 1919 Calgary Stampede's letterhead which Russell designed for its manager, Guy Weadick.

For Russell, the Canadian policeman was the prototype man on horseback. Cowboys and Indians he depicts both horse-borne and grounded; his Mounties are always mounted—but seldom in motion. Instead of action, there is tension, suspense. As K. Ross Toole so acutely observed about the artist, "again and again his theme was *portent*, not action." Nowhere is this characteristic more evident than in Russell's Mountie pictures. We ask, not What's Happening, but What comes next?

In "The Talk Paper," the constable is examining a document obviously presented by an Indian who, with his family, laden horses, and unencumbered

dog is en route—where? What is the talk paper? Probably a pass from the Indian Agent to permit the wayfarer temporarily to leave his reservation, perhaps to visit relatives among the Montana Blackfeet. Will the policeman allow the family to go on their way, or has the pass expired, and will he send them back to their reservation?

Two pictures show a Mountie on horseback with a drawn rifle enforcing the Queen's peace. In "Single-Handed," can he compel the Indian warriors to surrender the wanted miscreant? In "Caught with the Goods," will the whisky smugglers make a break despite the ominously aimed carbine?

In "The Queen's War Hounds," a sergeant and two constables, accompanied by three native tracker-guides, are studying the spoor left by some fugitive. Will they keep on the latter's trail and capture him, or will he escape? The issue is in doubt, for the Mounties' motto is not and was not "Get your man," but "Maintiens le droit."

Whether one calls it anachronism or artistic licence, Russell in his Mountie pictures occasionally took liberties with history. Thus in discussion of "The Queen's War Hounds" (now in Alberta's Provincial Museum and Archives), J.L. Ross notes:

Using the Indian costumes as a guide, it seems that Russell was portraying an event that occurred early in North West Mounted Police

"Caught with the Goods"

history. The Indians are wearing buckskin and weasel pelts, indicating a continuing preference for traditional attire. Use of trade items is in evidence in the standing guide's coat. It is easily recognized as a Hudson's Bay point blanket. Floral beaded pad saddles were not common to the Blood or Peigan tribes of this area. It was possibly taken as booty in a battle with more northerly tribes, perhaps the Cree or Assiniboine. The squatting scout's rifle is spotted with brass studs, sometimes a symbol of war exploits and a testament to his prowess.

Although the Indians' costumes suggest earlier years, Russell's Mounties are dressed as he saw them in the post 1900 period. Earlier, the scarlet dress tunics were doffed out of sight of the post, for the more familiar khaki or duck tan stable jacket. His men are wearing the stetsons which were not officially adopted until 1901. When the North West Mounted Police came to Alberta they still wore the pillbox hats as regulation gear. Due to the shadeless glare of the prairies, it was replaced by the cowboy type of hat.

Indeed, the only Mountie picture showing the pillbox forage cap is Russell's first, the one he did in 1885. This painting also depicts a realistically-limned buffalo skull at the lower left, presaging the conventionalized skull which later often became part of the artist's signature.

Not only did Russell continue to find artistic inspiration in the Canadian foothills land and people, he returned to Alberta a number of times. Thus the Calgary *Herald* reports that on February 21, 1903, he and Mrs. Russell were en route to Edmonton, and the same day, according to the Edmonton *Bulletin*, they checked into the Grandview Hotel in that northern metropolis. His stay was brief, as he left three days later. According to the *Bulletin*: "...his visit to Edmonton was for the express purpose of getting a drawing of a dog train from life." As there was none in town from the North, some friends—Russell had friends every-where—rigged up one so he could see it in operation.

Apparently the artist was surprised at the size of the centre, as the *Bulletin* reporter continues, "Mr. Russell was distinctly disappointed in Edmonton having expected to find a primitive fur trading post and instead found an up-to-date and progressive town."

When his friend Weadick organized the original Calgary Stampede in 1912, Russell had his first exhibition outside the United States. Billy Henry tells of Russell's cavalier attitudes towards prospective patrons:

In that year he had an exhibition in Calgary and had some beautiful paintings on show. He was never interested in selling them himself but always seemed to run them down. It was his wife who really sold them. I remember when he was talking to an Indian and someone came up to see about buying one of his paintings. Charlie said he was busy and told the customer to go see his wife.

With World War I (1914-1918) intervening, the second stampede was not held until 1919, but Charlie and his pictures were there. On that occasion, George Lane and a number of other wealthy Alberta ranchers purchased Russell's "When Law Dulls the Edge of Chance" as a gift for a young visitor, Edward, Prince of Wales. The price which Nancy Russell set on this work is reputed to have been $10,000. The Prince also took home another Russell, "Where a Left Handshake is Safest," as a gift from the Stampede Committee to the Duke of Connaught, great-uncle to the prince and a son of Queen Victoria. Retired in 1916 as Governor-General of Canada, Connaught had been guest of honor at the 1912 Stampede.

In 1920, the year the Prince was visiting Australia and New Zealand, Russell again crossed the Medicine Line, perhaps for the last time, to stage an exhibition in Saskatoon. But this was not his final Canadian showing. As recently as 1967, one was held in Edmonton by that city's Art Gallery.

The Canadian year, 1888-1889, was by no means lost or forgotten as far as the artist was concerned. It furnished him with an unending supply of artistic themes and subjects; it opened up a new public and new and expanding markets. But it did much more; it provided opportunities for new and enduring friendships. And finally, it led to full development of Russell's understanding and sympathy for this continent's native peoples, not only Blackfoot-speakers but Crows, Sioux, Crees, Stoneys (Assini-boines), and others.

No wonder Albertans like to claim a piece of Charlie Russell.

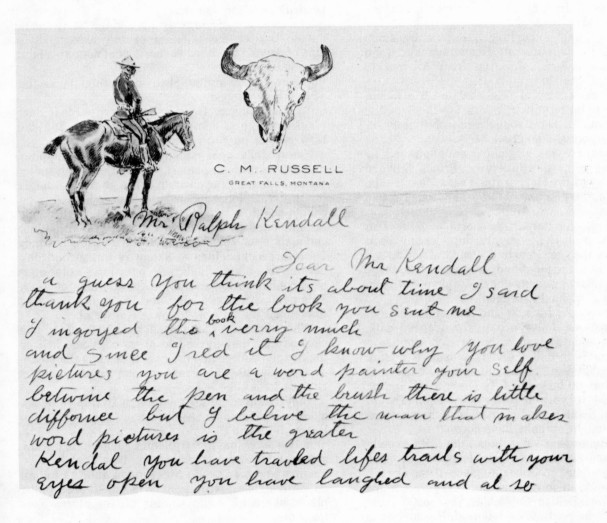

C. M. RUSSELL
GREAT FALLS, MONTANA

Mr Ralph Kendall

Dear Mr Kendall
a guess you think its about time I sand
thank you for the book you sent me
I ingoyed the book verry much
and since I red it I know why you love
pictures you are a word painter your self
betwine the pen and the brush there is little
diffornce but I belive the man that makes
word pictures is the greater
Kendal you have traveled lifes trails with your
eyes open you have laughed and al so

Portion of a letter to Sgt. Ralph Kendall, NWMP.

TO DAWSON OR BUST!

by Frank H. MacArthur

Canadian history contains many a thrilling chapter, but none more thrilling and interesting than the saga of three men from North River, Prince Edward Island.

More than half a century has gone by since Donald MacKinnon, Barrett Henderson and John Calligan took a herd of cattle from Alberta to Dawson City.

It was in the spring of 1898 that the trio began their never-to-be forgotten trek to the Land of the Midnight Sun. All were young men—physically fit. Only Henderson was married.

The expedition was originated and financed by Richard Heartz of Charlottetown, Prince Edward Island, father of the Honourable Frank Heartz who was the Island's Lieutenant-Governor from 1924 to 1930.

Learning of the desperate shortage of beef in Dawson City, due to the supply ships having been stuck fast in the ice, Heartz dreamed of sending a herd of cattle to the meat-hungry miners. Too, there was the chance of making considerable profit from the venture if it should succeed.

Prices were sky-high in the Yukon—a can of tomatoes cost one dollar, a can of condensed milk, two dollars and fifty cents, butter, five dollars a pound, sugar, one dollar and fifty cents a pound, while a breakfast of bacon with eggs old enough to vote cost four dollars and fifty cents at all eating places. Had it not been for the departure of hundreds of disillusioned gold seekers the previous year, some might actually have starved.

Barrett Henderson was to lead the little expedition with money and orders from Heartz to purchase sixty heavy steers in Alberta, place them on flat cars, and route them through the Rocky Mountains to Vancouver, British Columbia. The rest of the journey and the route to be followed, Heartz left to Henderson's discretion for he knew he could be trusted with great responsibilities.

The trio left Charlottetown with nothing but the clothes on their backs. One week later they were in Calgary, Alberta. The first leg of that never-to-be forgotten journey was over, but little did they realize the dangers, the heartaches and the hardship that lay ahead.

Henderson now made arrangements with the captain of a river boat to take the cattle to Skagway, Alaska.

Thus far, things had gone fairly smoothly, but the real challenge lay ahead—the badlands and quagmires to be conquered, the terrible blizzards and the bone-chilling frosts to be endured, the care of the valuable livestock—all added up to such a mighty challenge that few men would care to accept, regardless of the rewards.

The residents of Skagway advised the party not to go on. Due to the lateness of the season, their plan of driving the herd across a vast no-man's land was foolhardy.

"Winter here and start in the spring!" was the advice they offered.

To such advice, Henderson turned a deaf ear, MacKinnon and Calligan agreed that it was Dawson—or bust—and that was that.

Heavy sleds were constructed to carry supplies and the more docile steers were fitted to shoes by the local smith. These would serve as pack animals for the rest of the hazardous trip. When all was ready, the little expedition left Skagway, this time accompanied by a good cow dog, an Indian guide, and a none too reliable map of the district; but they were forced to return to Skagway the second day out due to a blinding blizzard, one of the worst ever experienced in the northland for the time of year. This caused further delay and the realization that they might not be able to make it after all.

When the storm had abated, the spirits of the trio revived and they agreed to press on, come hell or high water. Moreover, the cost of feeding the steers and themselves through a long, long winter would be ruinous to say the least.

They resolved to go on though it was now the month of October. Again their cry was: "To Dawson—or bust!"

A few days on the trail and another big snow storm hit the area. It caught the expedition in open country and big Donald MacKinnon and the Indian guide, Longboat, were sent forward to seek out a place where all could shelter till the storm blew itself out.

About two hours later the pair returned with good news; a small deserted shack, surrounded by a thick stand of spruce trees was discovered which proved

The residents of Skagway advised the party not to go on.

a godsend to the weary travellers.

The animals were secured to the trees and left in care of the dog while the men sought shelter in the shack with a couple of old mattresses and a quantity of hard tack and beans.

Meanwhile, the weather worsened, and over a week's delay was experienced before they were able to hit the trail again.

Progress was dishearteningly slow. Dragging the heavily laden sleds across the deep snow caused the lead animals much suffering. It was equally hard on the foot-sore pedestrians. Already they'd lost too much precious time but there was no turning back now for Old Man Winter was upon them.

Judging by their map and by Longboat's reckoning, a long distance lay between them and Lake Lebarge where poet Robert Service created Sam McGee. The trail led over half-frozen lakes, quagmire and long stretches of what Longboat said was the Devil's country. Henderson tumbled into a spring hole and would have most certainly drowned had not his companions rescued him. He almost froze before they could get him into dry clothes.

Their cry was: "To Dawson—or bust!"

Back in Charlottetown, Heartz began to have fears about the wisdom of sending three men on such a dangerous mission. He had received no word from the little party since they had left Skagway and the dread of their meeting with disaster disturbed him greatly.

The expedition moved forward at what appeared to the trio to be a snail's pace. And hungry wolves, driven half-mad from hunger, snarled at their heels. Twice within the next week, the herd was stampeded and more valuable time was lost in rounding them up. Worse still, nine animals were missing and presumed killed and eaten by wild beasts. Their loss was a bitter pill for Henderson as it would cut a deep wedge into his profit. It also put a damper on his pride for he had hoped to reach their destination without the loss of a single steer.

After many more weary miles of trouble, the expedition entered a snowless region where the soil was covered with dry grass. They camped and rested while the herd filled their bellies with the half-dried fodder.

Twice within the week the herd stampeded.

This country looked like the Promised Land after what they'd been through. Nearby was an Indian encampment whose menfolk trapped when not employed in helping the gold seekers over the famous Chilkoot Pass. The Indians proved a friendly lot and prepared for the seedy-looking whites the only good meal they'd eaten since leaving Skagway. To show his gratitude, Henderson ordered a steer to be slaughtered and this was their final feast until they reached Dawson City.

The next stopover was Tagish where a couple of Royal Canadian Mounted Police officers were on hand to look them over and to stare wild-eyed at the sight of so many cattle and so few men in that vast land of nowhere.

The Mounties told Henderson that it would be impossible to get the herd over the Pass.

"Your best bet," said one, "is to bypass the mountains and strike out for the Yukon River. Where you go from there is your problem. We hope you make it!"

Henderson's diary gives the date of the party's arrival at the river as the fifteenth of April. It was here they parted company with Longboat and Henderson consulted his partners regarding their next move and the three decided that a couple of large rafts might be the solution to their problems. It took another two weeks to build the rafts and by this time the river was almost free of ice.

Finally, the eventful day arrived. The remaining animals were driven aboard, followed by the three daring Islanders, and the voyage down the Yukon was underway.

Speaking to this scribe about the voyage, Donald MacKinnon observed:

"Once we lifted anchor, we just took things cool and floated along like a dream ship!"

All the town turned out to get a glimpse of the filthy, unshaven men and a couple of rafts loaded with contented, cud-chewing steers—a sight that pleased the town folk, many of whom had not eaten a good steak in months.

The forty-nine steers—all in remarkably good condition considering their long, hard trek—sold for one hundred and twenty-five thousand dollars, a large sum for those days.

"Why not try your luck in the gold fields?" cried a number of the miners in town to whoop it up. The answer was "No." The three had had their fill of adventure for the time being at least. They proposed to give Dawson City the once over and then return to Prince Edward Island, the place they knew and loved best.

"By pass the mountains and strike out for the Yukon River."

The night before their departure they were wined and dined and introduced to such famous persons as Robert Service and Klondike Kate. Then they left the city of eighteen thousand souls, never more to see its wild night life, or look into the sad faces of miners who didn't find the rainbow's end and the pot of gold. The trail of '98 had proved too rough for their tender feet. Only the young and the strong and the lucky won the race, for it has been said that in one year alone, forty million dollars was spent for outfits, food and transportation, while the output of gold for the same year amounted to but eleven million dollars.

From Dawson, the trio travelled to St. Michael's by steamer, a distance of eighteen hundred miles. The fare per man was three hundred dollars, and they were obliged to sleep on the deck surrounded by stacks of luggage and bad-smelling passengers.

The fever of the gold rush still ran high judged by the hundreds of people waiting at St. Michael's for passage to the Yukon.

After refueling at Unlaska, the party spent another six days on the Pacific Ocean before their ship anchored at Seattle, Washington. A brief stop-over and the trio entrained for Charlottetown, the last leg of that eventful and amazing journey which took eight months to complete. A journey well worthy of inclusion in the annals of Canadian history.

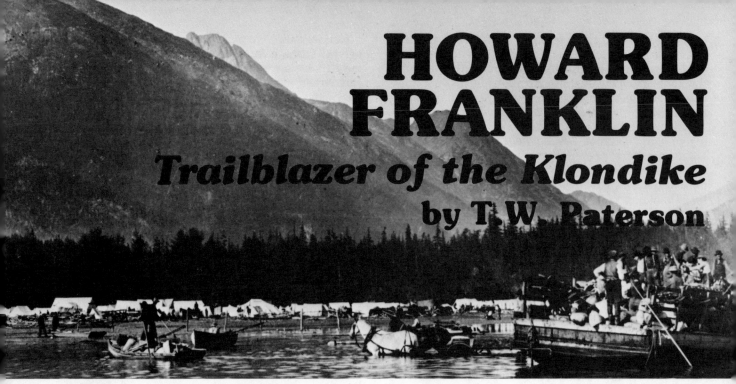

HOWARD FRANKLIN
Trailblazer of the Klondike
by T. W. Paterson

"The pathfinder for Bob Henderson, for George Carmack, and for all other past, present or prospective claimants of the honor attached to the discovery of the Klondike gold field:" This was Howard Franklin, unsung prospector and pioneer whose contribution to the world's greatest ever gold rush remains largely unrecognized, some three-quarters of a century after.

Even upon his death, 75 years ago, Franklin's claim to fame went virtually unrecognized. Yet it was Howard Franklin, noted the Victoria *Daily Colonist*, who "made the discovery of coarse gold at Forty Mile, and it was the finding of coarse gold at Forty Mile that brought about the exploration from which resulted the bursting of the Klondike with its dazzle of untold wealth of yellow dust and nuggets, upon a waiting world..."

Despite this fact, as the newspaper mourned, "Until his death Howard Franklin was practically unheard of. Even in his own country, he was without particular honor."

Whatever the case, Franklin's untimely passing marked the end of one of the more colorful careers in Canadian and American mining history. Born in Schenectady, N.Y., in 1843, he made his debut upon the Canadian stage a year later when his parents moved to Chatham, Ont., where Franklin remained for the first 29 years of his life. It was not until the age of 30 that the restless civil engineer answered the call of adventure and headed for California, land of the fabled gold fields. But the historic rush of '49 was long a part of history, and the California of the 1870s held little attraction for Franklin, and he decided to try his luck to the north. Once in Victoria, he went to work for the Canadian Pacific Railway, then making a preliminary survey for its proposed Vancouver Island link of the Transcontinental.

But railroad surveying did not hold Franklin's interest for long, either, and he soon chose the Cassiar and its booming gold fields. Restless and dissatisfied with the prosaic pastime of civil engineer, he turned to prospecting along the banks of Spruce Creek.

Mining was now in his blood, and soon the unexplored wilds of the North were beckoning to the former engineer and, in 1880, he moved on once more; this time to Juneau, Alaska. Three years later, having heard from Indians of gold in the Yukon Valley, Franklin, Tom Boswell and Henry Matherson headed into the hills in search of the "unknown Eldorado." It was a quest which Franklin would pursue for the rest of his life, help to change the course of history and, ultimately, cost him his life.

Shortly before his death, Franklin recounted details of that historic venture for a newspaper reporter. Their outfit, he explained, had consisted of "nine sacks of flour, 100 pounds of bacon, 50 pounds of beans, 50 pounds of sugar, five pounds of coffee, 10 pounds of tea, 10 pounds of salt, also matches and other small necessities, including baking powder."

These were the minimal supplies, supplemented by fish and game, upon which the three adventurers existed for more than two months. But they forgot their spartan fare when, on a sandbar 20 miles below the Little Salmon River, one June day, they struck paydirt. Using a rocker, the trio made as much as $40 each in a day. Their total take for 10 days was $1,500; a respectable return for their labors in that pre-inflationary age.

"We then dropped down about five miles and cleaned up a like amount in a week on another bar," said Franklin. "We also worked two bars below this and got a little dust."

Continuing downstream, they reached the White River and poled upriver about 40 miles. But, by this time, the season was well advanced and they did not dare stay too long. Shooting three moose, they returned downstream, intending to spend the winter at Fort Reliance. Earlier, they had asked a passing Indian to take a note to Al Mayo, the storekeeper there, in which they requested that he save them an outfit.

On October 3, they passed the mouth of the Klondike, then thick with ice, and proceeded to Fort Reliance. Unfortunately, Mayo had bad news for them; he had received their note too late in the season to order their supplies, and had sufficient only to fill his own needs for the winter. He did have a small surplus of some commodities, but Franklin dismissed these as being indigestible and, with Boswell and Matherson, resigned himself to existing for a while longer on the few supplies they had left.

Of the stock they had packed into the hills, they now were reduced to a block of matches, two pounds of tea and five pounds of tobacco; Franklin describing the latter item as having been "something fierce. It could be used for chewing or smoking, would drive mosquitoes away, cause sudden death to animal or man, if taken for the first time. But it was mighty good then!"

They were joined at Fort Reliance by another notable figure of the northland, Joe Ladue, who just arrived at the trading post from what would become the site of Eagle City. The four made themselves comfortable for the winter, spending much of their time in hunting. One such expedition, in company of a party of Indians, was made up Bonanza Creek. The prospectors were more interested in filling their bellies with moosemeat and, at the time, gave little thought to the creek's potential as a gold bearing stream. Besides which, the future eldorado was deep in snow at the time.

However, with the spring thaw of '84, their thoughts again turned to prospecting, when the new partnership of Franklin, Matherson and Ladue poled up the White River. They investigated a stream which they named after Ladue, but without reward, and returned, dejected, to Fort Reliance in July. Matherson then joined up with a new arrival at the post, Mike Hess, and proceeded to the head of the Tanana. This venture, too, was unsuccessful and Matherson and Hess headed out of the bush by way of the White River, intending to join Franklin and Ladue at Mukluket. On their way out, they made a brief stop at Forty Mile, where, two years before, Ladue had told them, two prospectors named Kerr and Powell had found "prospects." Although Ladue said he had noted color for a mile upriver, Hess and Matherson found little to hold their interest and continued on to Mukluket.

There, with Franklin and Ladue, they boarded the steamer *New Racket* for the passage to Fort Reliance. Once at the fort, however, they learned that they were in for another lean winter, as the post's stock of provisions was small. Franklin's former prospecting partner Tom Boswell, with whom he had first packed into the Yukon Valley, and who also was wintering at the fort, offered an easy solution to their supply problem. Rather than have to go to all the trouble of making daily hunting forays, he suggested, why not rob the Indian caches?

A full 20 years after, Franklin's anger with Boswell was apparent. As he explained, the Indians had, up until that time, been very friendly with the white prospectors. It would not do, he said, for the whites to "injure them in any way."

Meeting for a conference, Franklin, Henry Math-

Jacob's Ladder was the name of this 1898 portage in the canyon near Sheep Camp enroute to the Klondike gold fields.

erson, John Fraser, Mike Hess and Joe Ladue discussed Boswell's proposal and, after a full discussion, came to the conclusion that "we must protect ourselves from any such occurrences." Accordingly, the men drew up a note, which was duly presented to Tom Boswell:

Ultimatum

If you are caught robbing Indian caches you will be shot on sight.

[Signed] Howard Franklin, Joe Ladue, Mike Hess, Henry Matherson, John Fraser.

"It seems rather cold-blooded to make such a statement," Franklin conceded to his interviewer, "but it was absolutely necessary for us to keep on friendly terms with the Indians and there was only one way to do it — punish by death anyone who would upset the good feeling that then existed."

As testimonial to the Stewart's increasing importance as a gold producer, Mayo and two partners had established a new trading post there earlier that year. But, with spring and a new mining season, Mayo decided to try prospecting himself. With Franklin, Moffatt and Matherson, he headed up-river for more than 200 miles. Poling and panning as they went, the partners found an occasional trace of color but nothing sufficient to keep them for long in one spot. By late August, they decided to head downriver.

For his own part, Franklin had resolved to salvage the remainder of the season by making a quick check at Forty Mile Creek. "I had been thinking ever since I had panned on Forty Mile to return there some day, and when I reached the mouth of the Stewart, I concluded to do so."

When he mentioned his intention to check Forty Mile, five newcomers to the Stewart agreed to accompany him for a more thorough examination. While two of the expedition scouted ahead, the others followed at a slower pace, methodically panning every sandbar they encountered. As Franklin noted, they "got prospects on every one." Seven miles up the creek, he was making 15 cents to the pan.

"It was on the evening of the 7th (of September)," he recounted, "that I left the camp and walked upstream about two miles. I found a place where the bedrock was exposed, and in a crevice succeeded in getting out a shovelful of dirt. When I panned this I was surprised to find that it had much coarse gold in it. I hastened back to camp and showed the boys what I had got. We weighed the prospect and if I am not mistaken it weighed a half an ounce, or about $8.50 as gold went in those days.

"This place was about 500 feet inside the American boundary line."

Yet, when the prospectors poled their way to the site of Franklin's exciting discovery, they were disappointed. Despite a thorough examination of the bar, they found no further color. Franklin, it seemed, had tapped its one and only treasure.

However, all were convinced that his pocket of nuggets could only mean that they were on the right track, and they continued upriver until, at another sandbar, they again made good prospects. In honor of the senior member of the party, they named the site Franklin Bar.

The Chilkoot Pass, man-killing route to the Klondike, resembled a white ant-hill as prospectors continuously made their agonizing trek up the ice cut steps of the mountain, most of them carrying supplies for the journey to come. Note tripods for the aerial tram which carried supplies through the air—for those who could afford this service.

Despite this honor, Franklin was unwilling to waste his time there. He took but a day to stake what he thought would be a good claim and, with Phil Brown poled farther upstream as Jim McAdams and Henry "Tuck" Lambert proceeded with their working of Franklin Bar. For all of Franklin's eagerness to push on, he and Brown were content with poling just a few miles above Franklin Bar before returning to the mouth of the creek, when they proceeded up the Stewart for supplies and to "let the boys know that we had found coarse gold on the Forty Mile."

By the fall of 1885, Franklin and John Fraser decided against another winter at Fort Reliance and poled up the Stewart River. There, they made camp for the winter and, with spring, were joined by five more prospectors from the "outside:" Dick Poplin, Pete Wyborg, Frank Moffatt, and Al and Hugh Day. Then all headed farther up the Stewart. Panning their way along, they continued for no fewer than 70 miles when, on a single sandbar, they hit paydirt. Steamboat Bar, as they named the gravel ledge, produced the impressive sum of $30,000 in dust and nuggets, and soon attracted other prospectors. Among these latecomers was the unforgiven Tom Boswell, who, shunned by the others, worked a claim by himself.

"...I cannot let pass the opportunity without impressing upon you the richness of this bar," Franklin told the reporter interviewing him. "When we started up the Stewart the warm weather had just set in, and we struck the bar just after the snow had disappeared, and had left the ground thawed, yet the river did not show a sign of breaking up. Before the ice did go out, we had cleaned up $30,000. It was a regular thing for each rocker to clean up...to $300 per day."

Amazingly, Steamboat Bar was not their only eldorado that season. Five miles downriver, their attention was drawn by a blazed tree trunk. Carefully inscribed in the bark was a message signed by five prospectors four years before. Franklin could not remember the men's names, but he did recall their terse record: "No gold here."

The blazed tree, he chuckled, "was at the head of an island, and about 20 feet from it was the only place that I ever saw gold in windrows. For a few days we rocked as high as $300 a day. Pans went from $1.50 to $2.00. We simply skimmed the top of the bar, for that was all that carried pay."

Then it was September again, and the approach of winter. Heading downstream, the prosperous prospectors made camp six miles from the Stewart's mouth and received an adequate supply of provisions from the *New Racket*. This winter, at least, they would not have to rely upon foul tobacco and moosemeat...

Actually, they owed the quantity and quality of their supplies to the farsightedness of the agent for the A.C. Co., who had kept a careful tally of the number of prospectors who headed up the Stewart that year. He then had ordered enough provisions to supply all through the winter. As it turned out, there was even more to go around than he had planned, as the larcenous Mr. Boswell, whose proposal to rob Indian caches had made him a social leper among the prospecting fraternity, left the river

in disgust. Only seven remained for the season: Howard Franklin, John Fraser, Frank Moffatt, Dick Poplin, Henry Matherson, Hugh Day and Al Mayo.

They returned to Franklin Bar. Franklin remained until the summer of 1888, when, anxious for a change of scenery, he sold his latest prospect, a claim in the newly-worked Franklin Gulch, for $900. Thus unencumbered, and feeling flush, he headed for the bright lights of San Francisco, where, in short order, he squandered all of the gold for which he had worked so long, and so hard, in the Yukon and Alaskan Wilderness.

Then, broke but satisfied, he went back to work. But this time, instead of the Yukon, he chose British Columbia's Cariboo district, and, in due course, Washington and Oregon. By 1897, he was back in the Cariboo and, as before, deeply involved in mining. It was then that he, as well as the world, was staggered by reports of a sensational gold strike in the Klondike, Immediately, Franklin made arrangements to return, but, due to his involved interests in the Cariboo, he was unable to get away until the following year.

Alas, his return to the Yukon was too late. The man who had been among the leading pioneers to prospect the Yukon-Alaska boundary country profited little by the resulting stampede which was to become the greatest gold rush of them all.

Yet Franklin was not bitter. He had enjoyed half a lifetime of seeking the pot of gold at the end of the rainbow. As he explained, the coarse gold which he had recovered from Franklin Bar "was given to Harper and Mayo, who dispatched Williams and an Indian to Dyea, the former to San Francisco, to tell Jack McQuestin (their partner in the trading post) about the find that had been made. They left Stewart December 3, and were caught in a storm on the summit. Williams died of exposure and the Indian had a narrow escape, only reaching Dyea under great difficulty. Men went to the summit, got Williams' mail, and at a miners' meeting it was decided to open the letters and see what news had been sent out.

"In one, reference was made to the coarse gold, and upon its being found on Williams' body the news spread, and was the direct cause of the stampede which followed shortly after, and which did more than anything else to open up the Klondike country..."

Then, within months of his interview, Howard Franklin, prospector, pathfinder and pioneer, belonged to the ages. Characteristically, he died with his boots on, prospecting right to the end. While fording Bonanza Creek, he lost his footing and was washed some 300 feet downstream before fighting his way clear of the rapids. But the icy chill of the river and his exhausting struggle with the current proved to be too much for the 61-year-old miner, who died days after of pneumonia.

With Franklin's untimely death, after "many vicissitudes of fortune," a newspaper noted: "There passes one of the historic figures of the Newer North, one of (the) striking personalities in the history of the Yukon; one of the last of the picturesque 'old brigade' of Western mining camps..."

BIBLIOGRAPHIES AND SOURCES

SITTING BULL: Prophet or Pariah:
by Barbara Kwasny
Brown, Dee. BURY MY HEART AT WOUNDED KNEE. Bantam Books, Toronto, 1972
MacEwan, Grant. SITTING BULL: The Years in Canada. Hurtig, Edmonton, 1973
Northrop, Henry Davenport. INDIAN HORRORS: or Massacres by the Red Men. J.F. Hill, Augusta, Maine, 1891
Praus, Alexis A. A NEW PICTOGRAPHIC AUTO-BIOGRAPHY OF SITTING BULL. Smithsonian Institute, Washington, 1955
Vestel, Stanley. SITTING BULL: Champion of the Sioux, University of Oklahoma Press, Norman, 1957

FIRST IN THE WEST
by Doreen Mierau
Charters, Dean. MOUNTIE.
Haydon, A.L. RIDERS OF THE PLAINS.
MacGregor, James G. A HISTORY OF ALBERTA.
Chambers, Captain Ernest. RCMP
Atkin, Ronald. MAINTAIN THE RIGHT.
Denny, Sir Cecil. THE LAW MARCHES WEST.
Horral, E. PICTORIAL HISTORY OF THE RCMP.
Sharp, Paul. WHOOP-UP COUNTRY.

METIS TRIUMPH ON THE MISSOURI PLATEAU
by Hal G. Duncan
MacLeod, Margaret & Morton, W.L. CUTHBERT GRANT OF GRANTOWN.
Russenholt, E.S. THE HEART OF THE CONTINENT.

FREDERICK DALLY: Pioneer Photographer
by Joan Bellinger
British Columbia Provincial Archives
Files of the Victoria Colonist Newspaper

SAMUEL ZIMMERMAN: From Prosperity to Tragedy
by Pauline A. Pottelberg
Brown, George W. BUILDING THE CANADIAN NATION, J.M. Dent, Toronto, 1958
Tait, George E. ONE DOMINION. Ryerson Press, Toronto, 1962
Andreae, C.A. A HISTORICAL ATLAS OF SOUTH-WESTERN ONTARIO. author, London, Ontario, 1972
Glazebrook. A HISTORY OF TRANSPORTATION IN CANADA: Volume II. McClelland & Stewart, Toronto, 1964
Snell, J.B. EARLY RAILWAYS. Weidenfeld and Nicolson, 1964

THE "TALLAHASSEE": A Fighting Ship
by Eugene L. Hamm
Nelson. ATLANTIC READER.
Raddall, Thomas. WARDEN OF THE NORTH.

THE AGONIZING DEATH OF THE DUKE OF RICHMOND
by Vera Fidler
Dept. of Mines and Resources: National Parks Bureau, Lands, Parks, and Forest Branch. THE DEATH OF THE DUKE OF RICHMOND. Ottawa.
Walker, Harry and Olive. CARLETON SAGA. 1968

CANADA'S FIRST PLAY
by Janet Craig-James
Jeffery, C.W. A PICTURE GALLERY OF CANADIAN HISTORY: Volume I. Ryerson Press.
Bond, F. Fraser. AMERICA'S PREMIER 'FIRST NIGHT' Dalhousie Review.
Cameron, Margaret M. PLAY-ACTING IN CANADA DURING THE FRENCH REGIME. Canadian Historical Review.

THE BATTLE OF FISH CREEK
by Victor Carl Friesen
Anderson, Frank. 1885: THE RIEL REBELLION. Frontier Books, Calgary, 1968
Black, Norman Fergus. HISTORY OF SASKAT-CHEWAN AND THE NORTH WEST TERRI-TORIES. Saskatchewan Historical Company, Regina, 1913
Howard, Joseph. STRANGE EMPIRE, James Lewis and Samuel, Toronto, 1974
Morton, Desmond. THE LAST WAR DRUM. Hakkert, Toronto, 1972
Turner, John Peter, THE NORTHWEST MOUNTED POLICE: 1873-1893: Volume II. King's Printer, Ottawa, 1950

DAREDEVIL IN A PETTICOAT
by Dwight Whalen
O'Brien, Andy. DAREDEVILS OF NIAGARA, Ryerson Press, 1964.
Stamford, Ontario Kiwanis Club. NIAGARA FALLS, CANADA (A HISTORY). Ryerson Press, 1967.

MICHILIMACKINAC: The Bloodless War
William Silvester
Zaslow, Morris (Ed.) THE DEFENDED BORDER: Upper Canada and the War of 1812.
Swayze, Fred. THE ROWBOAT WAR ON THE GREAT LAKES: 1812-1814.
Mason, Philip (Ed.) AFTER TIPPECANOE: Some Aspects of the War of 1812.
Hitsman, J. Hackay. THE INCREDIBLE WAR OF 1812: A Military History.

THE BRATTON KIDNAPPING
by Anthony Appleblatt
Horn, Stanley F. INVISIBLE EMPIRE: The Story of the Ku Klux Klan: 1866-1871. Paterson Smith Publishing Corporation, Montclair, New Jersey, 1969.
Miller, Orlo. A CENTURY OF WESTERN ONTARIO. Ryerson Press, Toronto, 1949
WHITE TERROR: The Ku Klux Klan Conspiracy and Southern Reconstruction. Secker & Warburg, London, 1972.

FORTS, FURS AND HENS
by E.L. Lifeso
McGregor, J.G. BLANKETS AND BEADS.

SLUMACH'S GLORIOUS GOLD
by Brian Antonson
Antonson, R.A., Trainer, M. and the Author. IN SEARCH OF A LEGEND: SLUMACH'S GOLD. Nunaga Publishing Company, Vancouver, 1972

CHARLES M. RUSSELL: The Year in Canada
by John W. Chalmers
Adams, R.F. and Britzman, H.E. CHARLES M. RUSSELL: The Cowboy Artist: A Biography.
Gorman, R., E.G. GREAT WESTERN ARTIST CHARLIE RUSSELL. Golden West, Volume 13, 1968.
Many other sources, available on request from the publisher.

BOOK REVIEWS

COLUMBO'S CANADIAN QUOTATIONS
Edited by John Robert Columbo
Hurtig Publishers—Edmonton—$15.00

And the Lord said "John Robert Columbo, take unto thyself the honorable task of recording everything of worthy note uttered or written by a Canadian or about Canadians. Place these gems between two solid covers fully three inches apart, and cast your creation upon the populus, that they might see they do indeed have a culture. And John Robert Columbo did as he was instructed, for in his eyes it was a good thing, and the Lord smiled, for in his eyes it was a good thing, too."

The volume is entitled "Columbo's Canadian Quotations," and for those of us who have ever wondered what we Canadians think of ourselves and what others think of us—it provides an excellent mirror. Quotations about Canadians, by Canadians—having anything at all to do with Canada and its people—fill the 700-plus pages of the book. James De Mille's "Sweet Maiden of Passamaquoddy" finds immortality on page 146. On page 373 we find that George McCullagh once coined the phrase "I have no politics. I am a Canadian." And one page earlier we find that Colonel Robert McCormick, publisher of the **Chicago Tribune** said of our own beloved Newfoundlanders "They are so inbred as to be half-witted." No worry—he was merely tiffed that his plane had been delayed at Gander for four hours.

Words from the greater lips our nation has produced ("The law is a queer thing, I do not understand it."—Chief Poundmaker; "Fuddle Duddle."—Pierre Elliot Trudeau) and words from those of us more down to earth ("Some men, and all cattle, lack patriotism."—George Monro Grant; and "Tie off pancreas ducts of dogs. Wait six or eight weeks. Remove and extract." These words—scribbled by Sir Fredrick Banting on awakening from a dream, led to the isolation of insulin six months later.)

Whimsy, philosophical ramblings, political comment, great writings, great speeches, unrestrained praise, and angry denunciation—all can be found in "Columbo's Canadian Quotations"—at $15, a most worthwhile addition to any collection.

GABRIEL DUMONT—THE METIS CHIEF AND HIS LOST WORLD
By George Woodcock
280 pages, illustrated
$8.95 cloth
Hurtig Publishers

Gabriel Dumont was born on the prairie where he spent his childhood and adolescent years leading a semi-nomadic life around Fort Pitt, Saskatchewan. His happiest moments were lived during the excitement of the magnificent communal hunting expeditions for buffalo, which provided the Metis with food and clothing. But with the death of the buffalo herds and the stabilization of Metis society, created by priests' parishes, settlement became inevitable.

Woodcock's documentation of Gabriel's fight for Metis land rights and ascent to leadership is a powerful story: it parallels in many respects the fight by native Indians.

Gabriel's life centred around Batoche and St. Laurent, Saskatchewan, where he farmed and operated a ferry. It was in St. Laurent that Gabriel first set up a town council, whose purpose it was to create laws and restrain the mass buffalo slaughter. After years of futile efforts in bringing Metis grievances before an arrogant and disinterested Ottawa parliament, the Metis exploded in anger. Louis Riel, who was living in his Montana refuge, was persuaded to share his political knowledge and experience with the Saskatchewan Metis. The relationship between Riel and Dumont, and the battles at Duck Lake and Fish Creek in 1885 may surprise many readers, for Gabriel was truly a hero in his own right. He was a selfless man—completely concerned with the welfare of his people. He sacrificed his own homestead and material goods for the cause. Politically adept he was not, but a military genius he was. His small army of ill-equipped and haggard men doggedly supported him knowing full-well what the odds were against fighting the government police, and won.

Interesting too, is the role the church played in the breakdown of the Metis struggle: Riel and Dumont were both deeply religious men.

Woodcock has introduced almost too many names and characters—for this reason you may want to read his book twice. He is to be congratulated for bringing to light a significant study of a Canadian whose story seemingly has been hidden for too long.

THE LIFE OF LOUIS RIEL
Dr. Peter Charlebois
256 pages, illustrated
$7.95 paper, $14.95 cloth

Dr. Charlebois' extensive research into the life of Louis Riel, leader of the Metis during the late 19th century, is reflected in this hard-hitting documentary. He has elaborately chronicled the Metis' dire circumstances which led to Riel's leadership. Peripheral but important characters, including priests and government officials are boldly presented.

Charlebois has spared no mercy in his attack on Sir John A. Macdonald, Prime Minister of Canada. The actions of the Canadian government in dealing with the Metis on many occasions were dispicable. A reader could justifiably reprimand some writers of some Canadian school history texts for their bias in reporting the facts on the Metis uprising.

"The Life of Louis Riel" can be recommended for its two different approaches in enlightening Canadians about its government, and its heroes.

PEOPLE FROM OUR SIDE
A LIFE STORY WITH PHOTOGRAPHS BY PETER PITSEOLAK AND ORAL BIOGRAPHY BY DOROTHY EBER AN INUIT RECORD OF SEEKOOSEELAK—THE LAND OF THE PEOPLE OF CAPE DORSET, BAFFIN ISLAND
166 pages, 125 photographs, map
$12.50 cloth, $8.95 paper
Hurtig Publishers

Peter Pitseolak's book is hauntingly beautiful—his language and style are refreshingly simple. The original manuscript, written in Eskimo syllables when he was 70 years old, is a social history of the people of the Hudson Strait.

Pitseolak was a remarkable man, for not only was he a skilled artist, carver, author, hunter and fisherman, but he was the first Eskimo photographer to record daily life. He began taking pictures in 1942, developing them in igloos, tents and huts. The photos presented here date from the 1940's—mid '60's (the last days of the camp system) and are mainly portraits of family and friends.

The Eskimo traditions and customs Pitseolak writes about are fascinating. For example, bigamy and wife exchanges were a common practise until missionaries arrived.

Several of his stories centre around the arrival and departure of whaling and supply boats. Fortunately for the reader, "People from Our Side" is sprinkled with dozens of Eskimo words and their comparable English meanings. What may interest many Canadians who live south of Cape Dorset, particularly urbanites, is the Eskimo philosophy such as these examples from the book:

Two white men were found dead. An Eskimo who tried to take the clothing from one was stopped by his mother. She told him "These clothes belong to this man. If he were living he would not give them to you. Don't take them now he is dead."

In another instance, Pitseolak writes: "People didn't 'do' work until the Bay came here. Since they got paid, they liked it."

It is the 'old ways'—times before the white man—which Pitseolak so fondly remembers and which he has so brilliantly captured here.

CANADIAN BATTLES AND MASSACRES
by T.W. Paterson
Stagecoach Publishing Ltd.
208pp., hardcover (8½x11); $15.95

The ninth book by this B.C. author, **Canadian Battles and Massacres** is by far his most ambitious project to date; as it is that of the Langley publishing firm. National in scope, unlike Paterson's previous efforts which have dealt almost exclusively with subjects of British Columbia locale, this handsome "coffee table" volume covers almost three centuries of warfare in Canada.

And warfare there has been, although most Canadians must be unaware of the fact. For those of us born and raised in this century, Canada's military experience has been limited to the two world wars and Korea. For that matter, school history courses have done little to show that Canada, co-owner of the longest undefended border in the world, has, like almost all nations in history, suffered one bloody conflict after another. Tribal rivalry, French-English warfare, Indian "massacre," terrorist border raid, and a genuine revolution: all have occurred, with what might seem to be surprising regularity, on Canadian soil. Although North America's original inhabitants had long practised inter-tribal warfare, it remained for the arrival of the first europeans to transform localized bloodletting into a continental battleground. It is one of the ironies of Canadian history that Samuel Champlain, a man whom historians regard as being of honorable intentions and generally peaceloving nature, actually sparked a years-long reign of terror during which uncounted men, women and children died, many of them terribly, when he helped his indian allies defeat the Iroquois with gunpowder.

Alas, Champlain's was but the opening round of a conflict which saw one atrocity committed after another, when France and Britain later encouraged their Indian allies to attack enemy settlements.

Interestingly enough, another man fired another round which had horrendous repercussions. The man was a 21-year-old surveyor named George Washington. His fatal shot, as it turned out, sparked the French-English struggle for possession of North America.

Times, happily, have changed; a fact vividly illustrated last summer when, during Her Majesty's visit to the Olympic Games and Eastern Canada, for the first time in more than a century—and in violation of a treaty signed with the Americans after the War of 1812—Canadian warships sailed on the Great Lakes.

NORTHWEST TO THE SEA
by Marjorie Wilkins Campbell
$12.50 cloth
Clarke, Irwin & Co.
230 pages, illustrated

This book is a biography of William McGillivray. As with so many Canadian pioneer personalities, all too little has been written about McGillvray and, as a result, students of our country's history are deprived of valuable material. No longer.

With the addition of valuable photographs and detailed maps, the narrative is very interesting.

McGillvray is known as the Chief Director of the fur-trading North West Company, but we now see him as an aggressive, often frustrated, clerk, bourgeois and agent.

Always concerned with the rival Hudson Bay Company, he fought fiercely and competitively to establish a strong and viable fur-trading company under his direction. The life of a director then was not as now, for he spent endless hours in discomfort while canoeing or facing the hardships of extensive portaging, in the act of managing his company.

The northwest corner of North America was first opened for both the fur-traders and the settlers by this company and largely under the drive and direction of one man—McGillvray. This is his story—well worth adding to one's bookshelf.

CANADA INVADED 1775-1776
George F.G. Stanley
A.M. Hakkert Ltd.
illustrated 186 pages
$8.95 cloth

This publication is part of an ongoing project in co-operation with the Canadian War Museum. It is the result of their stated objective to present a complete review of Canada's military past. However, the book is presented in such a manner that it in no way needs additional volumes to make it complete.

Two hundred years ago, our neighbours to the south were in the midst of a violent revolution. At that time, there was a military effort to incorporate Canada into an enlarged continental union. George Stanley's book tells the story of how the American forces were defeated at Quebec.

The author is thorough in an informing narrative. In the account of Benedict Arnold's march to Quebec, we are told of his desperate attempt to secure information on "the Disposition of Canadians, the numbers of Troops in Quebec....what ships are at Quebec...." A nameless Indian runner, trusted with a secret letter, turned it over to British Authorities, thereby revealing an American collaborator inside the walls of Quebec (the intended receiver) and also preventing strategic data from reaching Arnold's men.

Numerous maps and many photos from the period add to the books appearance, readability and value.

YELLOWHEAD MILEPOSTS—Route of the Overlanders
Richard Wright and Rochelle Wright
Mitchell Press
illustrated, $7.95, 251 pages, soft cover.

Where many of our modern highways whisk us along at great speed and comfort, early pioneers tried, struggled and failed in numerous attempts to make passage. The settlements they strove for or the places they failed to pass and stayed to settle have sometimes grown to modern cities—others have blown away with the prairie dust.

It was often over such planned routes, often chartered by anxious yet inexperienced explorers, that western Canada was settled. Travelling at todays high speeds, history is often passed with the blink of an eye. So it is that this book, Volume 1 of a two volume issue, is welcome. Much to its credit are the extensive write-ups on a mile by mile basis—designed for the traveler's easy reference and quick fact information. Less history will then be passed by unnoticed.

In their introduction, the authors explain the origin of the 'Yellowhead Route'.

"Historically there was no 'Yellowhead Route', at least not by that name. Initially there were a series of trails which began at Fort Garry and headed west across the prairies. The Carlton Trail, sometimes called the Saskatchewan Trail, began there and continued to Fort Carlton. From there it proceeded to Fort Edmonton, though this section was often called the Edmonton Trail. From Edmonton a trail ran west through the Yellowhead Pass to Tete Jaune Cache. Earlier routes branched at Jasper to head over the Athabasca Pass to the Columbia. From Tete Jaune most early travellers headed down the Fraser River, but a few headed south through the North Thompson country.

"The present Yellowhead Highway combines these early trails, including a new road to Prince Rupert, into a highway system. It is this route that is followed in Yellowhead Mileposts."

THE WANDERING YEARS
by J.B. Vaughn
Hancock House
250 pages, paper $3.95

As a youngster in the Thirties, J.B. Vaughn was faced with a broken home and no money. And so he joined the hundreds of thousands of men who rode the rails across North America, looking for work. This is where the book is at its best. What Vaughn describes beautifully is the lifestyle of the times: living day to day, sharing and helping neighbours, and the prevailing optimism that someday things would improve.

Always on the lookout for yard bulls (policemen) while tearing away heavy brown paper from grain cars to build fires with, a determined young Vaughn occasionally found employment in logging camps, farming or odd jobs. Fortunately he had a sense of humour which he needed to survive three days trapped in a box car, sleeping 'catch-as-catch-can' in a church hall, and the endless hitching on dusty roads. Six bits a day was a good salary, and if you weren't working it was surprising how long you could get by on smokes and coffee. The endless search for work and temporary shelters certainly exemplify the drama of the times.

The second half of **The Wandering Years** deals with Vaughn's prospecting years in the bush. He had nothing but bad luck and was disappointed time after time. Somehow, despite the hard times, his love of the wilderness and his friends comes through. He concludes his book with an urge forty years later to return to his prospector's cabin in the hills.

OTHER HISTORY BOOKS
FROM NUNAGA:

A Seagull's Cry
East Kootenay Saga
New Westminster:The Early Years 1858-1898
The Saga of Turtle Mountain Coal
In Search of a Legend: Slumach's Gold

For more information on these and other titles available, please write:

Nunaga Publishing Company Ltd.
12165 — 97th Avenue,
Surrey, British Columbia
V3V 2C8

OR SEE YOUR LOCAL BOOKSTORE.

SUBMISSIONS FOR NEXT YEAR'S CANADIAN FRONTIER BOOK ANNUAL

Authors with manuscripts providing true, factual, accurate and interesting stories from Canadian history (pre-dating 1900) are invited to send their material or outlines to:

Brian Antonson, Editor,
Canadian Frontier,
P.O. Box 157,
New Westminster,
British Columbia,
Canada
V3L 4Y4

Submissions should be 2000 to 3000 words in length and typewritten: double-spaced.

Photos, sketches and maps should accompany submissions. Only exceptional stories will be considered without such material.

Authors should include a complete bibliography and biography with their submissions.

CANADIAN FRONTIER
BACK ISSUES

Volume 1, Number 1
Treasure Ships of the Great Lakes; Treasure Hunting in British Columbia; Alberta's Lost Lemon Mine; The Iron Box of the Belleisle; Blue Mountain Cave; A winter Journey in 1861

Volume 1 Number 2
James Houston — First Man to Discover Gold?; Pillage of Fort Selkirk; The Waddington Massacre; Murder at Beaver Pass; Coin Shooting; The Great Sea Battle of 1697

Volume 1, Number 3
Loyalist House; The Nonsuch; Charles D. McKay and his Famous Family Tree; One-Ear Charlie Brown; Hedley and the Old Nickel Plate Mine; B.C.'s Biggest Bank Robbery

Volume 2, Number 1
The 1910 Tornado at Rosthern; Log of the Privateer "Dart"; The Haunted Tribe; massacre at Big Qualicum; The Mysterious "Red Paint" Indians of Newfoundland; The Bluenose

Volume 2, Number 2
The Plank Road; The Battle of Duck Lake; The Secrets of Sable; Countess of Dufferin; Blondin: Tightrope over Niagara; Wild West Days in Prince Albert; Colonel By's Big Ditch; Log of the "Dart" — conclusion

Volume 2, Number 3
Norfolk Witchcraft; Murder on the Range-land; Gabriel Dument's Ferry; The Evil-Tempered Explorer; Macnab: The Laird of Dundern; Laura Secord: Heroine of Upper Canada; The Battle of Batoche

Volume 2, Number 4
And They Shall Maintain The Law; The Flying Dutchman; Montreal's Irish Stone Recalls Coffin Ships; The Loss of the Royal Tar; Try a Metal Detector; Mennonites: 1874-1974; The Battle of York.

Volume 3, Number 1
Escape From Fort Pitt; The Search for Tecumseh; Poundmaker: Son of Crowfoot; Almighty Voice; Pioneer Adventurer Faced Shipwreck and Hostile Indians

Volume 3, Number 2
The Disasterous Spring of 1833; The Restless Tombs of Isaac Brock; The Silk Connection; Massacre at Mahone Bay; The Lost Patrol; They Couldn't Save the San Pedro

Volume 3, Number 3
Hubert Darrell: Forgotten Giant of the North; Petroglyphs: Mysteries of the Past; The Grumpy General Who Put Down the Riel Rebellion; Grog Shops; Ghosts of Michipicoten Island; Ghost Towns of Alberta

Volume 4, Number 1
The Great Bird Rocks; Ship Killers; The Nootka Sound Controversy; HMS St. Lawrence: White Elephant of Lake Ontario; The Baker Massacre; Fort Livingstone; The Man who Lost Canada: The Columbia River Line

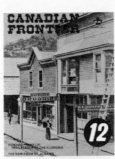

Volume 4, Number 2
Hell-bent on the Big Hill; Sole Survivor; The Mystery Skull; Howard Franklin: Trailblazer of the Klondike; The Raid on St. Albans; Disaster at Dejardins Canal.

Volume 4, Nos. 3 & 4
DOUBLE ISSUE: The Manitou Stone; The Shiners War; When Canada Fought the Fenian Raiders; The Disappearance of the Speedy; The King's Daughters; and 6 more.

These CANADIAN FRONTIER Back Issues are available for $1.00 each [$2.00 for # 13] from:

CANADIAN FRONTIER
P.O. Box 157
New Westminster,
British Columbia,
V3L 4Y4

INDEX